Geohistory, Capitalist Development and South Africa

Studies in Critical Social Sciences

VOLUME 310

Radical Geography

VOLUME 01

The titles published in this series are listed at *brill.com/scss-rgeo*

Geohistory, Capitalist Development and South Africa

From Racial Domination to Zim-Lite

By

Kevin R. Cox

BRILL

LEIDEN | BOSTON

The Library of Congress Cataloging-in-Publication Data is available online at https://catalog.loc.gov
LC record available at https://lccn.loc.gov/2024057505

Typeface for the Latin, Greek, and Cyrillic scripts: "Brill". See and download: brill.com/brill-typeface.

ISSN 2773-1928
ISBN 978-90-04-71557-8 (hardback)
ISBN 978-90-04-71558-5 (e-book)
DOI 10.1163/9789004715585

This book is printed on acid-free paper and produced in a sustainable manner.

In Memory of
Eleanor Cox
My Mother

Contents

Figures and Tables

Figures

Tables

Preface

I first went to South Africa in 1982, at the invitation of the South African Geographical Association. I was utterly staggered. I had never seen anything like it. But I was also fascinated. How could such complete, rigid racial segregation in all aspects of one's life have come to be? It was a total eye-opener. I visited Soweto and vividly recall the contrasts in housing with that of the white suburbs; also the smog that descended on the area mid-afternoon as coal fires were stoked up to prepare the evening meal; and this in virtue of the fact that at that time, most of Soweto lacked electricity. My hosts had a radiogram, as they were then called, but it was battery driven. I experienced what were then the homelands, the one-time native reserves, and the hostels for the migrant labor from those same areas. And around Durban and to the north of Pretoria, informal housing, shack dwellings that I had never experienced before. I was stunned by the contrasts, not just within South Africa, but between its third world aspects and what was typical of the US and the United Kingdom. The idea of a geography informed by racial differentiation and policy might be obvious, but it did not take me long to see that that would be short-sighted.

What made the difference were two things. Serendipitously, I was a subscriber to *Monthly Review* and one of their recent issues had comprised a (short) book length study entitled *The Crisis in South Africa: Class Defense, Class Revolution*, by John Saul and Stephen Gelb (1981.) This was a brilliant Marxist analysis of what was by then a very dynamic, politically fraught situation. So I was primed. I knew about migrant labor, I knew about influx control, the townships, the contradictory tendencies within Afrikanerdom and lots more; most importantly, I was inducted into seeing them in class terms and not the more obvious racial ones.

At the same time, seriously radical changes were underway in the South African academy. I remember very early on visiting a bookstore close to Wits University in Johannesburg and being surprised at what was available and eagerly buying: books like Marian Lacey's *Working for Boroko*[1] with the telling subtitle 'The Origins of a Coercive Labour System in South Africa'; and Colin Murray's *Families Divided* with the equally telling one of 'The Impact of Migrant Labour in Lesotho.' Even then, I realized that Lesotho was a *de facto* native, aka labor, reserve for South Africa. Particularly influential, though, would be Luli Callinicos's *Gold and Workers 1886–1924*, the first volume of her People's History

1 Meaning 'for nothing.'

of South Africa and published the year before my visit.[2] I recall devouring it one evening,[3] and learning about primitive accumulation, the white labor aristocracy, the logic of migratory labor and lots more that gelled with my growing appreciation of Marx. Yet just how and why South Africa is to be understood in class rather than racial terms, how race is mobilized by class interests and the circumstances of class dominance that facilitate the process has, again, been a work in progress.

Meanwhile, the library of books on South Africa and its peculiar historical trajectory has continued to grow and our ability to understand that country has undoubtedly benefited. There is, nevertheless, something seriously missing. There is what I call an internalist emphasis: that to understand South Africa we should prioritize events, processes and structures within the country itself. The view advocated here, and underlined by the reference to South Africa's geohistory in the title of this book, is that countries emerge and achieve their particular attributes, social, cultural, economic, within a global context that goes back at the very least to the dawn of capitalism; that, in particular, South Africa was molded by its insertion into an international division of labor that would require a very particular social structure – one already enabled by the racist discourse of European colonialism.

There are some other problems with the literature, but more contested. The most significant of these is the emphasis given to race. There are other interpretations more rooted in a language of class and accumulation, and which cast a more critical light on that emphasis. It is these that are favored in this book: the capitalist form of development has been *the* structuring force in South Africa, and it is its logics that gave race the salience that it acquired. Nevertheless, that form of development has to be cast in the context of its global character. The pressures on, and possibilities for, South Africa have always been of a global nature. And even while the first and second globalizations of 1870–1914 and 1970s onward left an indelible mark, the need to maintain a position in an international division of labor has been an insistent one ever since the discovery of gold on the Rand in 1996. These, therefore, are the touchstones of the interpretation provided in this book: a particular geohistory that extends well beyond the confines of South Africa and a capitalist one.

The book is dedicated in the first place, to those South African friends who first introduced me to a quite fascinating country: David Hemson, Felicity

2 It bears mention that all these books had been published in 1981, the year before my visit, and by a new, radical publishing company, Ravan Press. Happy coincidences.

3 Not that difficult since it had been written with a lay audience in mind and was copiously illustrated.

Kitchin, Jeff McCarthy, Brij Maharaj, and Mike Sutcliffe. Jeff read an earlier version and provided me with food for thought to which I hope to have done justice in the final one. I am very grateful to him. All five have always been generous of their time to no small degree on my frequent visits. Even while they might disagree with some of my interpretations, I could not have written this book without their support.

It is also, however, dedicated to the memory of my mother, and my South African friends will understand if it is she who takes singular pride of place on the dedication page. She was no paragon of racial justice but even she, by the early 80s, was referring to the Africans of South Africa as 'those poor people.' My gratitude to her is more general. Without her, I would not have been able to write *any* book. The daughter of a coal miner, her keenness for my academic success knew no bounds. I have little idea where it came from. But without her, I would not have had the encouragement, the access to books, and then the privileged schooling that opened doors that would then allow me to slake my curiosity about the world.

Finally, I would be remiss if I did not acknowledge events that occurred after the manuscript was submitted for publication. As indicated by the reference in the title to 'Zim-lite', my view of the immediate future of the country is not an optimistic one. At the time of going to press, the new coalition government in the country has seemingly generated new hope. This might seem to contradict the pessimistic tone of my final chapter. I see no reason to alter it. The structural conditions that have led to the country's present state remain in place and shifting them will be challenging, to say the least.

CHAPTER 1

Capitalist Development, Geohistory and the Peculiarities of South Africa

For the longest time, the country of South Africa was regarded as not just peculiar, but peculiar in an extremely undesirable way. This was because of a quite extraordinary racialization by white people or those sometimes ambiguously referred to as 'Europeans', and that was institutionalized by government fiat. Seemingly, race was the key to understanding everything about the country: it structured labor markets, it governed life chances, and in highly formalized ways. Race meant entirely separate ways of life: segregation in living places, in schools, in hospitals, even access to beaches and to post offices. The common understanding elsewhere was that this was a South African thing: a result of a politics internal to the country, and for which white South Africans were entirely responsible: a matter of government policy, certainly, but a government that enjoyed the strong support of the white minority, reflecting its privileged material position. The outside world simply looked on in disbelief. So, on the one hand, race was the key to understanding South Africa; and on the other, it reflected a politics both uninformed by, and resistant to, outside influences.[1] This book challenges both of these claims.

The racial structuring of social relations in South Africa was, as a few, largely of Marxist persuasion, have noted, a function of its peculiar capitalist development. All countries experience that development in their own particular ways. Not least, nowhere has some sort of 'difference' as it is now expressed, been absent; and even putting the all-pervasive gender difference to one side. It is a chronic feature of capitalist societies. Partly it is the desire of an emergent capitalism to impose itself through a discourse of superiority: that the lower orders are lower for good reasons, racial, cultural, upbringing, ignoble birth; and that their superiors are there to civilize them. This sort of discourse has been central to understandings of colonial expansion, but it applied equally to the original hearths of capitalist development themselves: the working class as an incorrigible 'race', drunken, feckless and improvident, and requiring

1 These are old biases, but they continue. A recent example is Edward Cavanaugh's (2016) article on South Africa as a settler colony. Not least, the idea that apartheid was overthrown from within, without reference to the Cold War and the frontline states, and no less a global economic crisis that bore down on the apartheid authorities, scarcely bears scrutiny.

 | DOI:10.1163/9789004715585_002

discipline of the capitalist sort if they were to make something of themselves. But then the insecurities of what it meant to be working class resulted in a jostle for survival, for recognition on the terms of a capitalist society, and a search for reasons to push others aside (Cox, 2021, Chapter 10.) Those of a different religion, culture, race, settler status, geographic origin, have all been stigmatized somewhere and at some time in the capitalist world, and it continues. Old forms of difference may be softened, but new ones will appear. Some of the edge of race in South Africa has gone but has been replaced by a sharp antagonism to Africans from elsewhere. But, and crucially, if it had not been race, it would have been something else. And in fact it was, as in the Xhosa/Zulu difference which would threaten negotiations about a new constitution in the early' nineties, not to mention Brits and Afrikaners. And always and everywhere, the 'respectable' and the 'riff-raff', or what were known in Victorian England as 'the dangerous classes.'

In addition, country-specific capitalist developments have always been global in their reach and in the way in which they have been conditioned, and as capitalism changed in all its different dimensions: technically, discursively, institutionally, geopolitically and through successive geographies, not least an ever-changing international division of labor and a fluctuating globalization. Everywhere it imposed limits, at the same time as it opened up new possibilities. This is not to claim any global form as a *deus ex machina*. It has been, rather, a case of a dialectic – bottom-up forces drawing on what was already in place: an ever-changing global space but in whose formations some countries have exercised more power than others.

In their development, across all dimensions of a social formation, countries should always be put in a global context. But for reasons of their specificity across those same dimensions, they can appear to be worlds unto themselves. This is misleading. While countries can indeed be regarded as totalities, if always under construction and reconstruction; they are also part of a world structured by capitalism. Apartheid may have been South Africa-specific, and it structured social relations in a very distinct way but, in virtue of a world sewn together by capital, it should be seen as a particular form of response to wider influences and conditions; just as in fact South African experience has had a more global impact – not least in the way in which the term 'apartheid' has been decontextualized and applied elsewhere. It is, in short, a concrete totality within an equally concrete one, both continually changing with the transformation of capital across all its moments and conditioning one another.

1 South Africa's Peculiarity

The peculiarity of South Africa referred first and above all to a quite extraordinary racialization of social relations; and then to the country-specific logic that was supposed to have brought it about. Racial hierarchy did indeed seem to permeate all areas of social life to a quite remarkable degree; something conveyed to the world outside South Africa not just by the media but by a distinctive literature stretching from people like William Plomer writing in the 1920s and 1930s all the way through to Andre Brink and Nadine Gordimer. Above all, of course, there was Alan Paton's hugely influential *Cry the Beloved Country*.[2] More ethnographic accounts like Elsa Joubert's *Poppie Nongena*, Vincent Crapanzo's *Waiting* and Richard Stengel's *January Sun* also had wide lay appeal.

This racialization reached a climax under apartheid, but it was already apparent earlier in what has usually been referred to as 'segregation' (Dubow, 1989). Race seemingly governed all areas of social practice, all social institutions, and, most importantly it privileged in material ways. Whites were always on top and Africans on the bottom. In between, with a little more privilege than the Africans, were the Indians and those who came to be known as Coloreds: people of so-called 'mixed race.' This applied to the country of South Africa, as it was constituted from 1910 onwards; and also to the colonies of the Cape and Natal and the Afrikaner republics of the Orange Free State[3] and the earlier South African Republic[4] which were to be brought together to create an independent country. There were changes. Informal racist practice gave way increasingly to state mandate. The racial structuring of society became more homogenized as the central branches of the state tried to rein in any tendencies on the part of local or provincial government that might threaten white rule as it saw it. It also penetrated into seemingly all areas of social life, reaching a climax during the apartheid years from 1948 to 1990.

Crucially, racial practice in South Africa imposed limits on the material possibilities open to the majority of the population. It is well known that over four fifths of the agricultural land of the country was reserved for ownership

---

2 Though there was also a subterfuge literature not so taken in by race like Alex LaGuma's *Time of the Butcherbird* or Wessel Ebersohn's *Store Up the Anger*.

3 Remarkably, from 1891 onwards, and by government fiat, Indians were banned entirely from living within the boundaries of the Orange Free State.

4 From the Treaty of Vereeniging that brought the Boer War to an end to 1910, the former Afrikaner Republics would be known henceforth as the Orange River Colony and the Transvaal respectively.

by whites. Business was almost entirely in white hands and government laws intended that it should remain so. The most remunerative positions available in the labor market were reserved for whites. As the country's occupational structure changed, then new positions might be opened up for the subordinate races, but always, whites had what was in effect, first pick. White labor unions were legal but African ones were not. The welfare state reinforced these structures of privilege. State spending on the education of white children was always vastly superior to that on African, Indian and Colored children. Prior to 1953 there were no schools at all for Africans other than those provided by the missions. Old age pensions were introduced but again, were calibrated to accord with the racial hierarchy. South Africa was – remains – a materially very unequal society and historically those contours of inequality always adhered closely to those of race. Tables 1 and 2 say it all. Whites were always at an advantage, and the rest seriously disadvantaged, though the Indians and the Coloreds slightly less so.

On the ground, in people's daily lives, much of this inequality was experienced as a quite extraordinary segregation. One thinks of apartheid in this regard but the pattern had been set, the precedents laid down, much earlier. Segregation occurred at all geographical scales imaginable. At the national scale, there was the division between the native reserves and 'white' South Africa. In the cities, the story was very similar, intensifying during the apartheid years when cities were required by law to separate the races strictly into their own distinct neighborhoods. Again under apartheid, and where the races might mingle, separate, racially exclusive facilities came into being, though often along European / non-European lines: as in separate park benches, separate railway station waiting rooms, separate hotels, separate schools, separate

TABLE 1 Racial inequalities under 'early' apartheid

	Africans	Coloreds	Indians	Whites
Expenditure per school pupil, 1953	180s.	408s.	408s.	1278s.
Infant mortality rate, 1958, per' 000 births	180.8	132.3	65.1	29.4
Old age pensions, 1960	261s.	894s.	894s.	2289s.

SOURCE: SOUTH AFRICAN INSTITUTE OF RACE RELATIONS 1959–60. MONETARY MEASURES ARE IN SHILLINGS PER YEAR

hospitals, separate post office counters, separate taxi cabs, separate sections of buses, separate railway carriages, and so on.[5] If the 'wrong' ambulance turned up at the scene of a highway accident it had to be sent back and the 'right' one called. However, one should be careful about drawing a hard line between apartheid and what preceded it. Separate white schools were always the rule. And like the Old American South, separate never meant equal. Racial inequality was inscribed in the landscape, insistently communicating inferiority to anyone who wasn't white. All of this meant, among other things, that movements were quite rigorously structured along racial lines. One proceeded from one's own racially exclusionary residential area, via the 'right' section of the 'bus, to go and sit in a park on a bench reserved for you, then use the correct elevator in a public building, subsequently proceeding to the counter for Europeans or not as the case might be, and so on.

Such for most of its existence was the peculiarity of the country of South Africa: a quite extraordinary set of racially structured arrangements, pervading all aspects of social life, and one which it was impossible for the visitor to overlook. But quite how might it be explained? To the extent that it was, then it was in terms of an internal social logic which privileged the role of the state in a racial struggle for material advantage. Some were better off and it was race that accounted for it. Whites had, through acts of legislation like the 1913 Land Act and job reservation, monopolized economic opportunity, leaving the scraps for the other racial groups. The colonial form of the state had facilitated this.

One of the more theorized accounts of this, by Kenneth Good (1976), tried to grasp it in terms of what he defined settler colonialism. This grouped South Africa along with other settler societies in which Europeans had been the minority: notably Algeria, Kenya and Southern Rhodesia. In all of these, the settler / colonized distinction overrode class differences among the settlers. South Africa was different again, though, because in the strictly formal sense it was an independent country; something recognized by the South African Communist Party in its designation of the country as a case of colonialism of a special type, and so simultaneously endorsing the sense of it as 'exceptional.'

It was, of course, with respect to a particular point of view that South Africa became defined as 'exceptional': notably a de-racialized vision of the world promised by decolonization and the virtually universal revulsion in the

5 Sometimes separation meant separation for the four major race groups. This was the case with beaches. For an excellent discussion of separate amenities under apartheid see Christopher (1994, Chapter 5).

TABLE 2 Racial inequalities under 'mature' apartheid

	Average monthly wage in manufacturing 1980 (in rand)[a]	Average monthly wage in mining and quarrying 1980 (in rand)[b]	School spending per pupil 1978–79 (in rand)[c]	Pupil-teacher ratios 1983[d]	Maximum social pensions/ Month (in rand)[a]	Life expectancy at 5 years[d]	
						M	F
Africans	237	172	71	42.7:1	33	55.8	61.8
Coloreds	273	318	225	26.7:1	62	52.8	60.1
Indians	307	439	357	23.6:1	62	59.4	63.2
Whites	979	1040	779.9	18.2:1	109	64.5	70.1

a For columns 1, 3 and 4, Smith, 1982, p. 27
b Wilson and Ramphele, 1989, p. 52
c Burman and Reynolds, 1990, p. 98
d Ibid, p. 28

developed world subsequent to Nazi genocide.[6] This was an exceptionalism that became more easily definable as white settler states elsewhere were toppled, like indeed those of Algeria, Kenya, and Southern Rhodesia; and then the successes of the civil rights movement in the US seemed to remove any barriers there to joining in the general disapprobation. This was so even while actions, particularly Western investment in South Africa, spoke louder than words; until, that is, the investment environment deteriorated to the point at which some compromise had to be brokered. In short, South African governments discovered that they could not work against the current of a capitalism that was global in its structure. South Africa was, after all, even fundamentally, a capitalist country.

6 Though curiously not so much those of the Japanese, even though the latter had a finely developed sense of racial superiority.

2 Putting South Africa in Context

In trying to make sense of this, I take it as axiomatic that the capitalist form of development should be the ultimate point of departure, along with all of its abstract determinants. Not least these would include the class relation, cost competition, the industrial reserve army of labor, the division of labor both between and within firms, and incessant accumulation: all following from the original separation of immediate producers from the means of production. To that one should add a state that acts to reproduce the capitalist status quo and facilitate its expansion, and then the fact of difference. As indicated earlier, I would insist that the latter is a chronic feature of capitalist development: embedded in its logics of domination and the inherent insecurity of the working class, even while its concrete shape has been variable and subject to displacement by still others. The same applies to the idea of country.[7] The capitalist world is geographically fragmented into discrete territorial forms that can be regarded, if deceptively, as worlds unto themselves: as enjoying a unity, as in fact, expressing a totality of forces, and resistant to external forms of regulation, other than that of the world market and even that, judging from the history of globalization, subject to some modulation.

The contradictions at the heart of capitalism, the resistance of labor, a chronic tendency to overproduce, then means an ongoing transformation of all aspects of the social process: technological, organizational, geographic, changes in the division of labor, in what is produced – everything, but always in concrete ways that do not infringe on the fundamental logic of extracting surplus value. On the other hand, in no way can this transformation be regarded as a random walk. It is not just that change moves in tandem affecting all aspects of the social process. Concrete change at one point in time provides a condition for what follows. There have, accordingly, been some distinct phases and tendencies.

Globalization is built into capital's logic; something vividly described in the Communist Manifesto. Earlier, there was a phase based on various forms of unfree labor in the Americas and elsewhere, including what we now know as South Africa, which would have later repercussions. Subsequently, globalization has been marked by a shifting tempo. There was an acceleration that lasted from about 1875 to 1914 that has been dubbed 'the first globalization', and

7 Hobsbawm talked about nations, but he might just as well have been referring to the less politicized idea of country: "Nations, we now know … are not, as Bagehot thought, 'as old as history'. The modern sense of the word is no older than the eighteenth century, give or take the odd predecessor" (1990, p. 3).

a more recent one from the late 1970s on: periods in which international trade and investment surged. In between, there was a long retreat into national confines that would start to ebb very slowly after the Second World War: a period from about 1950 to 1975 that some have referred to as capital's golden years and not uncoincidentally, apartheid's as well. There have then been shifts in the accumulation regime which only roughly map on to these changes: so a period up to the Second World war where states tended to be minimal both in their employment and in their interventions. Then the expansionary period of the golden years characterized by what has been known by some as those of the Keynesian welfare state and by others as Fordist. More recently, there has been some return to a less interventionist state through what has been called neoliberalism, though in no way a return to prewar conditions.

There has then been something that I want to call the long cold war, with the emphasis on 'long.' It is far too easy to reduce what is commonly called the Cold War to a struggle between states, whereas, what it was, particularly for the United States, was an anxiety about what its leading politicos called 'freedom'; which if you looked at it a little more closely, meant, quite baldly, the freedom to make money at the expense of others and to live in a state of permanent insecurity. In short, it was part of an attempt to make the world safe for capitalism and to relieve it of working-class challenge; something that would be met by a measure of success.

The anxiety, however, goes back much further in time. The high tide of the labor movement was actually in the years immediately following the First World War: this was a revolutionary period embracing not just the Russian revolution, but the abortive ones in Germany and Hungary, and signal events like the (British) General Strike of 1926. In a quantitative study, Beverly Silver (2004) has identified 1919 and 1920 as the peak years of labor unrest in the world as a whole.[8] This frightened ruling classes everywhere, into fascist reactions in some countries,[9] and then world war; a war initially fought with some hesitancy by Great Britain and the United States as they looked to Germany to defeat the Soviet Union and all that it stood for, and for labor movements everywhere. Through the seductions of the welfare state, their reformist wings would triumph over the revolutionary, and then pave the way for their utter collapse after Thatcher, Reagan and the implosion of the Soviet Union. The implication for the South African ruling class was that ceding formal power to the African National Congress (ANC) would no longer seem so cataclysmic.

8 A period, actually 1920–1924, which corresponded to the peak of electoral success for the South African Labour Party.

9 For example, Graham (2005) and Traverso (2016).

But it would also leave the ANC bereft of the ideological resources necessary to resist the blandishments of the West, its 'international' institutions like the International Monetary Fund (IMF) and its armies of 'advisors.'

This long decline of the labor movement, part of labor's real subsumption to capital (Aronowitz, 1978) maps only roughly into that other great sea change which has been the displacement of formal empire. Granting independence to former colonies promised openings for the left but hopes that were to be disappointed. The US fretted about communist takeovers, particularly after the experience with Cuba and Vietnam, but the worry was exaggerated. Empire and subordination to capital on a global scale have asserted themselves in new ways. South Africa is a classic case. The revolutionary aspirations of the ANC were never particularly strong, and in the negotiations, the Western advisors did not have to try very hard.

3 South Africa and the Global Political Economy

These global forces and conditions interacted with ones internal to what would be South Africa to lay the foundations for its particularity. In so many ways, what transpired in South Africa since the time that it could be defined as such, echoed more global developments. Table 3 is intended as suggestive, showing how in many respects South Africa has tended to march in tandem with the rest of the world, how it has slotted into wider, more global structures like those governing international exchange, the international division of labor, empire, or indeed the tensions around uneven development and the Cold War.

South Africa as we know it today was to a striking degree a child of the first globalization. But before that there was a phase that would prove crucial to the way in which it would experience it. Like much of Latin America, the Caribbean, and the American South, early development would be based on unfree labor; in Latin America and South Africa, this would continue till quite late with serious repercussions for the development process. Incentives to develop the productive forces would be weak, so that to the extent that industry took off it would be hampered: inadequate supplies of food for urban populations; and, lacking major streams of immigration, shortfalls in the supply of labor. That this would play into the initiation of apartheid is indisputable but not widely acknowledged. Unfree labor would also contribute to racial composition and other parallels: so South Africa's Colored population, for which an essential condition had been the import of slaves into the Cape from Batavia and parts of Africa. Later, in the wake of the abolition of the slave trade, there

TABLE 3 Moving in tandem with the rest of the world

	Rest of the world	South Africa
THE MERCANTILE PHASE	* Exchange with indigenous peoples	* Ditto
	* Production, typically using unfree labor for export to Western Europe: cotton, sugar, tea.	* Slaves from Africa and the Dutch East Indies for the production of wine in the Cape; indentured workers from India to produce sugar in Natal.
FIRST GLOBALIZATION	* The rise of the neo-Europes	* South Africa as a neo-Europe
	* Outmigration from Europe to the neo-Europes	* A surge of white settler numbers in South Africa
	* The rise of the Old International Division of Labor	* SA as a producer of raw-materials
	* Empire and colonialism	* The colonial character of SA
	* The pervasiveness and taken-for- grantedness of racism	* Ditto[a]
	* The gold standard	* SA as major producer of the world's gold
	* The rise of the labor movement and White Laborism	* 'Workers of the world unite, and fight for a white South Africa'
THE GREAT RETREAT	* Have Nots vs. Haves (Germany, Italy, Japan vs France and Great Britain)	* Afrikaners vs. English speaking whites
	* Drawing the fangs of the labor movement	* Ditto[a]
CAPITAL'S GOLDEN YEARS	* Fordism	* Racial Fordism
	* The incorporation of the working class	* The racially differentiated incorporation of the working class
	* Urban and regional planning	* Apartheid as a form of urban and regional planning
	* Decolonization	* The homeland project ('Grand Apartheid')
	* Neo-colonialism	* The homelands as neo-colonies

TABLE 3 Moving in tandem with the rest of the world (*cont.*)

	Rest of the world	South Africa
THE SECOND GLOBALIZATION		(PRE-TRANSITION)
	* The fiscal crisis of the state	* The fiscal crisis of apartheid
	* De-regulation	* Abolition of job reservation and influx control
	* The Cold War	* SA as the West's proxy in Southern Africa
		(POST-TRANSITION)
	* Dismantling trade barriers	* Ditto[a]
	* Privatization	* Sale of municipal utilities and of state-owned enterprises
	* Liberalization of capital controls	* Ditto[a]

a 'Ditto' is to be read horizontally and not vertically

would be indentured labor: the principal reason for South Africa's Indian population and those of the Caribbean.

The first globalization would then be the period in which the outlines of what is now known as the Old International Division of Labor first became clear: a division between the producers of industrial goods, largely in Western Europe and North America, and producers of raw-materials, often colonial in character, on the other. It was a division of labor whose instantiation owed much to the freeing up of international investment subsequent to the adoption of the gold standard; investment that equipped the raw material producing countries with the physical infrastructures which would be necessary if they were to function as part of a global system of production and exchange. At the same time there was a massive outpouring of white people from Western Europe to the American and Canadian West, the Antipodes, and what have been called more generally by Alfred Crosby the Neo-Europes:[10] a migration

10 Through the term 'neo-Europes' Crosby (1986) designated those parts of the world in which the climate was such as to sustain an agriculture supporting a European diet and which were the destinations of Europeans during the great migration from Europe in the latter part of the nineteenth century and only coming to an end with the outbreak of the First World War.

that provided the necessary labor power if this global project was to be accomplished.

South Africa was an important, perhaps crucial, part of this. Gold was discovered in 1886 and precipitated major investments in railroads, ports and urban infrastructures in what was, until 1902, a pair of British colonies and two independent Afrikaner republics, and thereafter, until union in 1910, four colonies. The area became one more destination for Europeans. White miners quickly became unionized and contributed to the spike in worker militancy so clear in other parts of the world prior to and immediately after the First World War. They also shared with workers elsewhere in the empire a tendency to what Jonathan Hyslop (1999) has called White Laborism. The combination of fierce resistance to employers and racism was not a monopoly of South African miners, but one shared with the Australians and the British. In Australia the Labour Party was the principal source of pressure for the White Australia policy introduced in 1901. In Great Britain in the 1906 election, the Labour Party lent support to the demands of white miners in the Transvaal for an imperial ban on the sponsored immigration of Chinese for work in the mines: a curious expression of the solidarity of labor. There were clear traces of these influences in the American Chinese Exclusion Act passed in 1882.

Yet by the 1930s class as an explicit form of political cleavage around the world had receded into the background and had yielded to more territorialized forms of consciousness; part of the ruling class reaction to the challenge of revolution. The collapse of demand in the global economy led to savage competition for world markets, a retreat into autarky and a renewed struggle for empire. Germany, Italy and Japan demanded a redistribution of imperial possessions; they defined themselves as the Have-Nots in contrast to Great Britain and France (Dutt, 1936).[11] In South Africa this form of national contestation was internalized as the struggle between a fierce Afrikaner nationalism and the more privileged English-speaking whites with their supposed loyalties to the British Empire. The right wing of the Afrikaner national movement looked to Nazi Germany as its savior. Their interest was not in new territory but in the existing territory of South Africa, control of which they believed had been taken away from them by the British: the Treaty of Vereeniging of 1902, which brought the Boer War to an end and established British ascendancy in South Africa, seemed to parallel German humiliations at the Treaty of Versailles.

---

11 http://archive.spectator.co.uk/article/27th-december-1935/7/the-claims-of-the-have-nots- (Accessed July 7, 2024).

British defeat in the war would, it was anticipated, result in a reordering of the country's national hierarchy constituted by Brit and Boer.[12]

After the Second World War we can see the same sort of parallelism. The South African government embarked on a radical program of social engineering. Western European notions of city and regional planning were put to new racialized purposes (Parnell and Mabin, 1995): the sharp segregation of land uses, including residential areas; and later the redistribution of employment away from congested cities in ways that mimicked the attempts of Western European countries to relocate employment away from major urban centers to areas of relative unemployment (Romus, 1958). In other instances the government felt pushed. Without decolonization elsewhere in Africa it is unlikely that it would have embarked on the homeland project.

In short, it is hard not to be struck by the various ways in which the conditions for change in South Africa – or resistance to it – have been global in character. It is impossible to understand the events leading up to the overthrow of apartheid except in the context of globalization, albeit in its capitalist form. I would argue that far from having a contingent effect, as some have argued, the global character of capital was a necessary condition. As in other countries tied to the rest of the world through significant exchange relations, South African business experienced the same decline in profitability that occurred elsewhere after the early 1970s. There was a global contraction in world markets resulting initially in what was known then as a fiscal crisis of the state, paralleled in South Africa by the fiscal crisis of apartheid. Neoliberalism or what was being defined as 'globalization' would be embraced in the rest of the world as a crucial part of the solution (Harvey, 2005). De-regulation became a buzz word, and in South Africa this meant dismantling core elements of apartheid like job reservation and influx control. Both had long since gone before the transition to a non-racial franchise.

For the South African ruling classes, the global has been both a limit and an opportunity, ever shifting. The first globalization, lasting from about 1875 to 1914 opened up possibilities for the development of a distinctive niche in the international division of labor, and this would be hugely consequential for the making of modern South Africa. In short, the more global has been constitutive of the changing character of the country: an essential aspect of its being and becoming, therefore.

12 At that time Africans seemed, relatively at least, irrelevant. The racial question in South Africa had been defined in the 1930s as one in which the contending parties were those of British origin and the Afrikaners: remarkable, and testimony to the relative political quiescence of people of color at that time.

Everywhere, these global transformations and tendencies were refracted in quite particular ways by ruling classes that confronted different sorts of opportunities or constraints and acted in ways limited and facilitated by their own highly particular geohistories. This was no less true of South Africa. For a start, there were distinctive forms of uneven development, marking off capitalist cities from countrysides where pre-capitalist residues were still evident. In part, this was a question of the African reserves that would play, in virtue of the access to land enjoyed by all married males, a crucial role in securing the migrant labor for the gold mines.[13] In part, it was a matter of a white countryside where landowners, dominantly though not exclusively Afrikaner, lived off the labor of share-croppers, aka 'squatters', and of labor tenants: those granted access to some land in exchange for immediate labor. These were largely African, but not entirely.

This uneven development would factor into economic and political change in distinctive ways. A delayed agrarian revolution meant that for a very long time there was a chronic shortage of labor in the country; which helps to explain why the mines recruited extensively in Southern Africa as a whole and at one time looked as far afield as China. The countryside, moreover, was dominantly Afrikaner. There had always been a drift to the towns, but this accelerated greatly during the 1930s, creating a moral panic in the Afrikaner establishment, but also an opportunity. For in the cities, particularly those of the Rand, they entered at the bottom of the white stratification system (Grundlingh, 2019): so ideal material for an Afrikaner nationalism bent not only on reinforcing traditional values of church, family and female purity, but in gaining power on a program of mass uplift, even while at the expense of the majority of color.

South Africa was also unique among those settler colonies with a settler minority, and therefore susceptible to the demands for a non-racial franchise. The size of its settler population, its industrial capacities, gave it an unusual ability to resist those demands, and it did so for longer than anywhere else. Industrialization, even while limited, meant that it could resist Western sanctions fairly comfortably. It had technical capacities that could enhance that self-sufficiency even further; the development of the oil-from-coal industry is an important instance. And it had its own military and was not dependent on

13 We should also note that without a substantial African population, with limited historical expectations regarding a standard of living, exploitation of the gold, occurring at depth and of low grade, would have been impossible. This cannot be taken for granted. In the Americas and Australia, the indigenous populations were decimated by the diseases brought by the Europeans, but that was not the case in Africa.

the support of an imperial power in resisting demands for an extension of the franchise that would encroach on settler privilege.

Algeria provides a useful contrast. Prior to French cession of an independent Algeria, the European population was not much less than that in South Africa at that time: about 15% vs 19%. But they had to rely on the French army and even if the attempts at a settler coup in 1961 had succeeded, they would have lacked South Africa's industrial capacity to continue the struggle. During the 1920s and 1930s, even into the 1940s, South Africa's racial state had not seemed that unusual. It was only with struggles for independence, Cold War anxieties about leaving the field open to the communists, and the successes of the civil rights movement in the US, that it would start to stick out like a sore thumb. But it had the capacity to resist.

It was and remains within this shifting juxtaposition of conditions and forces, that the class struggle in South Africa would unfold, but not in any predictable way. It would be mediated by what the critical realists have called 'structures of social relations' (Sayer, 1984, pp. 92–96): relations between people, drawing on conditions of time and place, to empower, and so confront the contradictions of development in South Africa. These would take the more concrete form of coalitions pulled together and given leadership by a variety of forces ranging from the Chamber of Mines in the late nineteenth century; through to the Afrikaner National Party that would dominate for just over forty years; to the ANC as it struggled to impose cohesion on the forces opposing apartheid; and opposed as they would be, by a Zulu nationalism mobilizing migrant workers in order to sow mayhem and weaken the ANC's bargaining position. All of these forces were enabled by particular geohistoric conditions.

Gold would be the foundation of modern South Africa: a launch pad into its industrialization in the broadest sense. This would eventually include agriculture as a branch of industrial capitalism and source of surplus value. In virtue of the gold standard, there was a bottomless market for gold, but there were other conditions that had to be in place, and the lead would be taken by the Chamber of Mines. They agitated for British intervention in order to displace what they experienced as the hostile policies of the (Afrikaner) South African Republic.[14] They would then create a set of conditions that allowed them to make money in the unpromising geological circumstances of South African gold: so migrant labor drawing on Africans with limited expectations, and whose wage demands would be further circumscribed by the Chamber's

14 Not to be confused with the Union of South Africa, which did not come into existence until 1910.

exercise of a labor hiring monopsony; and then the importation of mining skills from North America and Western Europe, but which would require their incorporation into the ruling coalition. The outlines of apartheid were being put into place.

What would bring it closer, courtesy of a radicalized National Party, was a mix of conditions. These would include the confrontation of the modern, intensified by the urbanization of Afrikaners, and the traditional that would at the same time, animate European fascism; the challenge to patriarchy, to moral certainties and to the rule of the Dutch Reformed Church – the National Party at prayer, as it was called. But the National Party agenda was also a response to to the post-war crisis of urbanization as a creeping permanent settlement of Africans took place, threatening the mines with militancy and wage demands, and white farms with labor shortage.[15]

But if apartheid seemed to be an answer to the contradictions of the earlier settlement in which the Chamber of Mines had played the leading role, its own contradictions would be the beginning of the end. The attempt to whiten South Africa by expelling the majority of Africans to the soon-to-be-independent 'homelands' would, through sheer material necessity, convert the occasional migrant worker into a permanent one, paving the way for the rise of worker militancy and the independent African unions that would have the overthrow of apartheid in their sights. A shortage of skilled workers would then result in the training of young urban Africans and an enlargement of those numbers most likely to be politicized; one result of which was the Soweto riots of 1973. In the 1940s and 1950s, the National Party had relied on the racism of the rest of the industrial world to implement its system; but this racism was long in question and it now had to struggle against the threat of sanctions, all in the context of the stagnation of the global economy that had set in, in the 1970s. The balance of political forces was shifting, but how it would be perceived and acted on – a matter of race, or of class – would be decisive for the current conjuncture, as we will now see.

15 It is also well known that the National Party could never have triumphed in 1948 without a malapportionment at the time of the creation of the Union of South Africa in 1910, designed to salve the wounds of the Afrikaner population.

CHAPTER 2

Creating 'A Country'

1 Introduction

If there is a pivotal date for the coming into being of the country we now know as South Africa, there are compelling reasons for choosing 1886. It was then that gold was discovered in the area now known as the Rand, stretching in a line east and west from what would become the city of Johannesburg. The discovery was hugely consequential. Without it, it is doubtful that there would have been a modern South Africa in the way we came to know it or that there would have been the transformations that have marked its history more recently. What is now South Africa was then an area of relative backwardness and of political fragmentation, even inchoateness. There were two colonies, those of the Cape and the Natal, that were something of backwaters in the British Empire; and two independent Afrikaner republics, the South African Republic and the Orange Free State, which, from the standpoint of the world economy were even more irrelevant, lacking anything that could compare to the wool exports from the Cape or the sugar exports from Natal. The development of gold mining would change all that. This is because it would unleash a process of far reaching economic, social and political change, incorporating the broad mass of the population into the channels of value circulation on a global scale, introducing large scale production to the sub-continent, and inciting a process of political unification that would result in the creation of one country: the Union of South Africa.

From a more global standpoint, the date '1886' is also signal, since it falls into the period corresponding to what has since become known as 'the first globalization.' Making its presence felt from about 1875 on, this was a complex process that created new growth possibilities in the world economy, rising on the back of the gold standard, steamship navigation, and empire: largely formal empire but also informal as in the relations between Europe and some of the Latin American countries like Argentina and Uruguay. It brought to an end a period of depression in the European economy, over-accumulated capital spilling out to take advantage of new investment opportunities in North America, particularly its Western provinces and states, the Antipodes, some of the Latin American countries and South Africa. The result would be the first discernible international division of labor: the exchange of capital and consumer goods from the eastern states of the US, and Western European countries, particularly

 | DOI:10.1163/9789004715585_003

Belgium, France, Germany, Great Britain, the Netherlands and Sweden, for the raw-materials and agricultural goods of Latin America's Southern Cone, the western parts of North America, Australia and New Zealand, South Africa, and to a lesser degree Western Siberia, West Africa and South and Southeast Asia.

Through gold, South Africa would prove to be an essential part of that international division of labor. This was because of the gold standard. Without the gold standard the massive European investments opening up the western regions of North America, Latin America's Southern Cone, the Antipodes and continental Russia in particular, would not have happened, simply in virtue of currency risk. The problem with the gold standard was that the supply of gold put a limit on the money supply and hence the rate at which accumulation could occur. The exploitation of South Africa's gold would reduce those limits and allow some mitigation of deflationary biases in the world economy. In an important sense modern South Africa was a child of the first globalization, and a crucial child at that; a major contributor.

Yet despite the propitious global circumstances, it can fairly be said that the development of gold mining initially hung in the balance. The geology of the gold deposits was far from encouraging. While the deposits were huge, and in fact would provide South Africa with a dominating position in world production for almost a century, large amounts of rock had to be mined in order to obtain a relatively small amount of gold. For the most part they occurred at great depths below the earth's surface, necessitating extremely expensive capital investments if they were to be mined. In terms of the potential 'gold mined per worker' and 'gold mined per capital sum invested' the prospects were daunting. Something had to give if the business was to be profitable and it would be labor costs. This would have crucial implications for the country's history and its tortured racial politics.

Geology was not the only problem. The gold was located in the (Afrikaner) South African Republic. For the Republic's government, the discovery of gold was a mixed blessing. On the one hand it welcomed the possibility of taxing the industry in order to develop the country's agriculture and promote industrialization. On the other, it feared both the competitive pressures the industry would impose on the country's rural labor supplies and the British domination of gold mining. The major gold mining companies were British, they imported British engineers and they imported British labor to perform the more skilled aspects of mining. This created the problem of the uitlanders, or outsiders, what to do about them in terms of political rights, and the danger that the Afrikaners would become a minority in what they had regarded as a redoubt immune to British influence.

Eventually there would be a political and institutional fix that would facilitate the rise of gold as the major export of a newly united country but imposing it would lead to lasting and consequential resentments and it cannot be said that everything was in place before the mid-1920s. The early years of the industry were to be ones not just of experimentation as the Randlords, as the mine owners became known, sought solutions to their different problems – securing labor, securing a friendly political regime – but also of resistance, some of it violent.

None of this took place on a tabula rasa. Agrarian institutions, neither those prevailing in those parts of the country where European farmers had appropriated the land, nor in those where Africans had successfully resisted them, were propitious to the implantation in their midst of capitalist forms of production. The gold mining companies needed wage workers and very large numbers of them. But Africans enjoyed access to land both in what was coming to be known as the native reserves and on European farms; in the latter they were either sharecroppers or they worked for the European landowner-farmer in exchange for access to some land. In consequence, they had limited interest in wage work.

Mention should also be made of what Mahmoud Mamdani (1996) has called the bifurcated state. This was a colonial creation in sub-Saharan Africa dividing colonies into areas of direct rule in which Africans and whatever white settlers there might be, were directly subordinated to a European colonial government acting according to civil law and to institutional arrangements that were thoroughly racialized. Notably Africans did not have the vote. The bifurcation came from the fact of areas of indirect rule in which Africans were subordinated to the rule of chiefs and customary law. The colonies of the Cape and Natal conformed to this pattern, one eventually to be extended to the former Afrikaner republics. This too would be foundational for creating the sort of country that South Africa would become.

The remainder of the chapter opens with a discussion of the first globalization and how it related to developments around gold in South Africa. This is followed by a discussion of the problems faced by a nascent gold mining industry: problems which reflected in part the geology of the deposits but also the historical legacy of what would become South Africa. This was a legacy created by various comings and goings, conflicts and institutional sedimentations. The problems were simultaneously technical, economic and political and would have to be resolved by the creation of some sort of institutional fix. This slowly comes into being but cannot be said to have been thoroughly in place until the 1920s. It would then give the gold mining industry what it needed in the form of a country, a 'structured coherence' in Harvey's terms, to establish itself as a profitable part of a division of labor on a global scale. But by the 1940s, this fix, in some of its essential aspects, was being called into question and was coming under serious political challenge; which meant in turn that South Africa's position in the international division of labor was being threatened. This set the scene for apartheid which managed to clamp things back into place, at least for a while. This will be discussed in the chapter to follow.

Finally, and before proceeding further, we should note that little so far has been said about race. Race will, of course, figure prominently in the particular set of institutions that emerge to protect South Africa's place in the international division of labor as a gold producer; in fact it will be fundamental. It will also be a crucial part of the discourse that comes into being to justify them. What I wish to emphasize, though, is that the more basic pressures emanate from the capital accumulation process and the class tensions it enjoins. The making of modern South Africa is also the making of its racial composition, of the meanings of race there, and the tensions that it generated and continues to generate. A politics of race was prior to gold but the capitalist development process unleashed by gold mining transformed it into something far more virulent and ultimately, hard to marginalize. I will take this up further at the end of the chapter. The fundamental point, though, is how race condenses out of pressures that ultimately are more global in character, that reside in the nature of accumulation as a global process; just as the selection in of race as a legitimate way of dealing with those pressures is likewise not something that can be reduced to a South African exceptionalism irrespective of more global discourses about difference, not to mention the pressures conducive to it in general.

2 The First Globalization and South Africa

Developments in the last fifteen years of the nineteenth century in what would come to be the country of South Africa were part and parcel of what some have called, and in contrast to the most recent round of globalization, 'the first globalization.' This was a period of concerted growth in the global economy resulting from the emergence of the first clearly defined international division of labor in the world: one that related the industrialized economies of Western Europe and the Northeast and Midwest of the US to raw-material producing areas around the world, and in particular, in the Southern Cone of South America, the Antipodes and the Great Plains of North America.

Overaccumulation in Western Europe had resulted in declining profitability and what has come to be known as the long depression lasting from 1873 to

1896, though it was experienced particularly severely in Great Britain, where it coincided with challenges to British industrial supremacy from Germany and the US. The discovery and exploitation of new frontiers of capitalist development around the world would facilitate a suspension of this barrier, while also bringing about changes in the British economy, which would be important for events in South Africa. Attention focused in particular on what have been called 'the neo-Europes' (Crosby, 1986). These were those areas in the world which approximated in their climatic conditions to those of Europe and to which a European agricultural complex of plants and animals could be relatively easily transferred. They included, therefore, the Southern Cone countries of South America, the Great Plains of North America, Australia and New Zealand, a thin sliver of Western Siberia, what would come to be known as the Baraba steppe, and much of what would be South Africa where the high plateau would be an important moderating influence in the area's sub-tropical latitudes. These would become major sources of raw-materials and foodstuffs for Western Europe and the cities in the eastern parts of North America with implications for industrial wages there and so for industrial recovery. On the other hand, the transformation of the Great Plains of North America, Argentina, Australia and Uruguay into, among other things, breadbaskets for Eastern North America and Western Europe required massive investments in physical infrastructure, particularly railroads. This provided one outlet for over-accumulated capital, and the fillip it gave to the expansion of iron and steel production was another. Meanwhile, subsequent agricultural depression in the 'old' Europe, fueled a massive outmigration to the 'neo-Europes.' Thus, were created the conditions for the first clearly demarcated international division of labor. Accordingly, the transformation of these countries during the first globalization is nothing short of remarkable (Table 4) The expansion of railroad networks is striking, and most of the increase in population was due to immigration from Europe and then the natural reproduction of the immigrants.

Global conditions were therefore ripe for capitalist expansion in the Southern African sub-continent if only a major commodity, resource or staple could be developed. In 1886 this would make its appearance in the form of gold. There had been something of a dress rehearsal for its exploitation in the earlier discovery of diamonds in 1867 in the Cape colony. This was a dress rehearsal in the sense of providing the opportunity to explore particular ways of creating and managing a dominantly African labor force; ways which would later influence the development of gold mining. It was also a demonstration of what was possible under the congenial circumstances of specifically British colonial rule. But despite the fact that it is often grouped with gold under the

TABLE 4 The first globalization and growth in the neo-Europes

	Railroad length (km)[a]		Population[b]		% Change population	Mean % change per year
YEAR	1870	1913	1870	1913	1870–1913	
ARGENTINA	732	33478	1796	7653	326%	7.6%
AUSTRALIA	1529	31453	1775	4281	141%	3.3%
CANADA	4211	47160	3781	7852	108%	2.5%
CHILE	732	8070	1945	3431	76%	1.8%
NEW ZEALAND	74	n.a.	291	1122	286%	6.7%
SOUTH AFRICA	0	14149	620[c]	1276[d]	106%[e]	5.0%
URUGUAY	n.a.	n.a.	343	1177	243%	5.7%
USA	85170	401977	40241	111401	177%	4.1%

a Bénichi, 2003, p. 24
b Maddison (2003)
c Figures are for 1891 for the Cape colony and Natal and for 1890 for Orange Free State and the South African Republic; figures are for whites only since there are no statistics available for all races for the South African Republic for either of these years. See Christopher, 2009, Table 1, p. 103
d 1911
e Calculated over the 21-year period 1890–1911 only

category 'the mineral revolution', it was small tea compared with what would follow.

The creation of a colonial geography followed in the wake of these developments: one connecting mines and agricultural regions via the coast to Western Europe and North America. Cape Town and Durban would be to Montevideo / Buenos Aires / Sydney / Melbourne / Montreal, just as the railroads extended up to the Rand had their equivalents in a dense mesh across the Pampas, the Murray/Darling basin, the Great Plains and the prairies of Western Canada. Indigenous populations had already been decimated, though significantly not in South Africa: 'significantly' since African miners were to be crucial to the profitability of the gold mining industry. Without them and their political vulnerability it is unlikely that, given the capital expense of mining gold in South Africa, it could have been a commercial success.

Great Britain, and above all, London, was a crucial nexus in this first globalization and would take an intense interest in South African developments. London's role was first and foremost financial: international banking, including the purchase of foreign bonds; the insurance of global shipping; and the financing of trade, since London performed important entrepôt functions with respect to much of Western Europe. Given the German and American challenge in manufacturing, the role of the City of London as the financial hub of the global economy was increasingly significant to the British economy as a whole. But under the gold standard, London's ability to finance trade and foreign investment depended on the gold it had at its disposal. Accordingly, the Bank of England was eager to purchase gold wherever it might be found, which lent additional point to the discoveries in South Africa and sharpened Great Britain's stake in creating an appropriate institutional context for mining there. It is to that topic that we now turn.

3 An Institutional Fix for Gold

3.1 *The Challenges*

The gold deposits discovered in the sub-continent in 1886 were located in the (Afrikaner) South African Republic or SAR (see Figure 1). The deposits were of vast magnitude, even more than was initially realized,[1] and promising huge scope for money making if the right conditions could be set in place. But this would turn out to be a big 'if.' The conditions – institutional, discursive and assembling the large numbers of workers that would be required – would indeed be created; but the resultant form of that particular set of social structures and practices would haunt the emerging country all the way down to the present day, where it continues to have remarkably powerful echoes.

There were two major issues and they were connected. The first was the challenge of profitably exploiting gold deposits where their geology demanded huge capital investments and large labor forces. The gold was at very considerable depths, requiring the sinking of expensive shafts, and the installation of ventilation and pumping equipment. The reefs also had a very low gold content, which meant that proportionally more workers were required to produce a given amount of gold. To aggravate matters, the mining companies would have no power over the gold price, and no matter what proportion of world output they were able to achieve. Rather the gold standard determined a fixed price. Profitability, therefore, depended on exercising downward pressure on production costs.

1 This would become very apparent later in the late 1940s with the discovery of yet newer fields in the Western Transvaal and the Orange Free State.

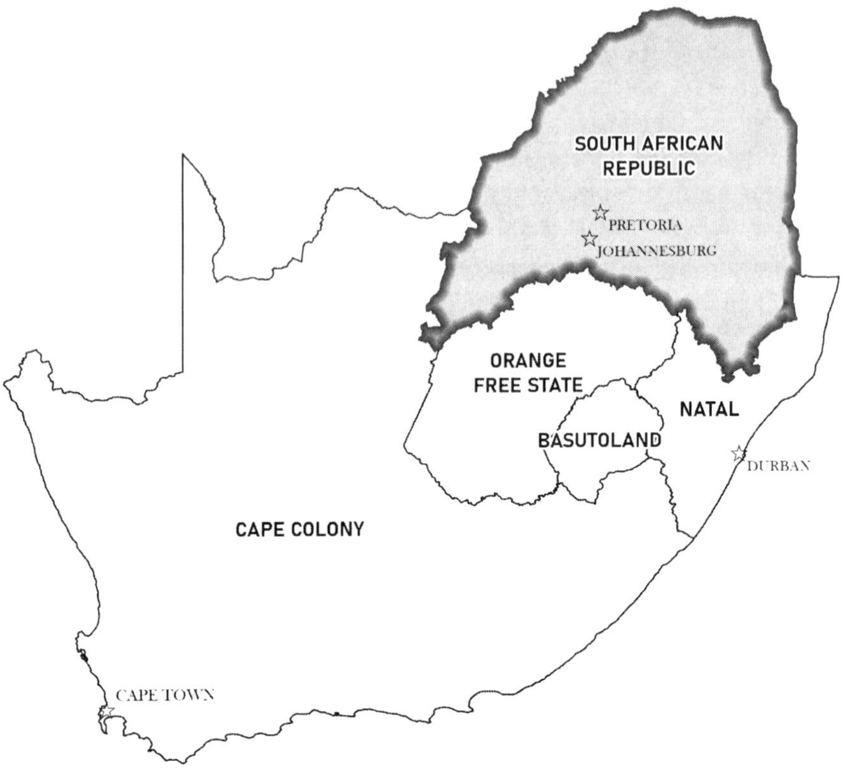

FIGURE 1 The South African Republic, 1899
MAP BY RUIXUAN DING. SHAPE FILES KINDLY MADE AVAILABLE BY BRENT MCCUSKER

From this standpoint, the fact that the initial discoveries were in the (Afrikaner) South African Republic (henceforth SAR) did not help. The SAR had its own agenda. Governing a dominantly agrarian society consisting of white farms whose production depended on hoarding labor, the massive labor demands of the mines were a threat, and there were attempts to ration labor. On the other hand, the mines were viewed as a cornucopia for the Republic and taxed accordingly; the intention was to turn those revenues to developing the country's economy. The fact that the mining companies were British-owned and the skilled workers required were English-speaking immigrants from Great Britain, Canada, the US and Australia made matters worse. Afrikaner / British tensions had a long history in the sub-continent. The creation of the two Afrikaner republics of the SAR and the Orange Free State had been subsequent to the movement of Afrikaners out of the Cape resulting from frustrations with British rule. In the second half of the nineteenth century there had been a number of abortive attempts to subordinate them once again. Mistrust hung heavy in the air. Not least there was the question of the so-called uitlanders or English-speaking immigrants and anxieties about being swamped and so, as they achieved political rights, being subordinated to the British through the backdoor. But the mines were unhappy and the British government had an important stake in ensuring that they should be profitable.

3.2 *The Fix*

The fix arrived at consisted of two elements: the subordination of the South African Republic to imperial rule; and the creation of a set of labor institutions and supporting discourses that would keep costs down and allow the profitable extraction of the gold. From 1902 onwards, the first condition is secured, but at the cost of an ongoing wound that would haunt developments in what would become South Africa for a long time to come. This is because it was secured by force; namely through Great Britain going to war against both of the Afrikaner republics in what became known as the Boer or South African war: a war that would last three years and yield a rich harvest of bitterness among the Afrikaner population, particularly in what had been the Afrikaner republics.

Initially the SAR and the Orange Free State (OFS) were converted into British colonies, with the SAR assuming the name the Transvaal and the OFS, the Orange River Colony. In an attempt to soothe the hurt, they were then brought together in 1910 with the other two British colonies of the Cape Colony and Natal in the Union of South Africa: the so-called marriage of (Afrikaner) maize and (British) gold. The resentment, however, would continue for a very long time indeed with important consequences for the trajectory of the new dominion as it was known. Not least, it would be one of the conditions, at least discursive, for the construction of Afrikaner nationalism during the 1930s and the desire of Afrikaners to make good their losses and get back 'their' republics. This would be important in the construction of apartheid after 1948 since by then, that would be the agenda of the principal vehicle of Afrikaner nationalism, the National Party.

This political drama would be played out against a background of quite severe labor scarcity. Creating a set of institutions that would secure labor for the mines at wages that they would be willing to pay had been a major preoccupation prior to the coming into being of the Union and would continue to be so for a very long time. By 1924 it seemed as if the problem had been solved. But it never was in any enduring fashion until the 1970s, and by then a different set of challenges were looming for the gold mines.

To repeat: In South Africa the gold mines needed very large numbers of workers and very cheap ones. As we have seen, the problems were largely geological but the fixed international price for gold did not help. This was so much the case that if supply and demand had determined wages there would have been no gold mining. Africans were simply not available for work in the mines in the numbers that would have held wage costs down. Rather South Africa was a country characterized by an extreme shortage of wage workers. There were two major reasons for this. In the first place, there was the backward nature of white agriculture, with the result that white farmers had substantial labor demands of their own. These were satisfied, for the most part, by granting Africans access to land on their farms. As explained earlier, what had emerged was a class of farmers-cum-landowners who relied for their surplus product largely on the labor of sharecroppers and labor tenants. There was some production for the market but a compulsion to revolutionize productivity on the land and so manage with fewer workers was generally weak. Any threat to livelihood from market limitations could be answered by a shift in the balance between production for subsistence and production for exchange. This meant that large numbers of Africans were locked up – almost literally, as we will see – on white farms and unavailable for work as wage workers in the mines. Certainly, the increased demand for foodstuffs with the rise of gold mining had begun to bring about change. There were capitalizing farmers anxious to produce more for the market and so interested in transforming their work processes and taking over direction of the labor process from their sharecroppers and labor tenants. There were also, however, farmers, possibly with larger amounts of land to allocate to labor tenants and sharecroppers, who were quite happy as they were. In consequence they were seen as an obstacle to what the capitalizing farmers would have called a more rational allocation of labor in the 'white' rural areas.

Second, there was the fact of African agricultural production itself. Married African males enjoyed rights of possession to the land in the native reserves, though not private property rights. As sharecroppers and labor tenants on white farms, they enjoyed access to land through contract with the white farmer. Most Africans lived in the tribal enclaves that either were already, or were to become, native reserves. Land was held in common. In addition, there were small colonies of land-owning African peasant farmers distributed across the 'white' rural areas. They too saw limited need to work for a wage, whether in the gold mines or elsewhere.

The solution hit on by the mines comprised a number of distinct but complementary elements. The first was an emphasis on migrant labor. The gold mines came early to appreciate the value of the migratory form for the large numbers of unskilled workers that they needed; a lesson learnt from the earlier exploitation of diamonds in Kimberley. They set up, through the Chamber of

Mines, organizations to recruit them, and bring them to the mines, not just from South Africa but from much further afield in Southern Africa as a whole. At the mines they would typically live in compounds, which facilitated labor control. This, however, only touches the surface of its significance. The major point was that the miners did not bring any 'dependents' with them. Rather they stayed behind in the rural areas, lived off the land, built their shelter 'off the land,' paid limited taxes for limited communal facilities, like roads or sanitary sewerage or schools, of which there would be very little. Accordingly, the reservation wage of the miner could be less.[2] His wage did not have to cover the needs of an accompanying family or the cost of urban housing, urban services and the like. This was the logic that underpinned the support of the mines for institutionalizing migrant labor through government legislation, particularly the influx control measures of the apartheid governments from 1948 on, which were so detested by Africans.[3] Permanently settled labor, however much Africans might prefer it, and increasing numbers of them did, remained anathema to the mining industry for a very long time.[4]

This is not to say that migrant labor had no attractions for the African. Most significantly, to all those inserted in a dominantly subsistence form of life, it meant money to pay the taxes that the state had imposed to try and push them into wage labor. For the capitalizing African peasant class – sharecroppers, some independent peasants on former white-owned farms, even some in the reserves – sending a younger family member to the mines for a nine-month contract or two could also mean money to buy improved seeds, equipment and livestock. Later, as patriarchy began to break down, it might give a son, through the money earnt, an opportunity to break with patriarchal control and sidetrack a father's permission to marry by purchasing his own bride wealth.

2 Bozzoli (1983) has suggested that African patriarchy and its characteristic division of labor was important here. Unlike among European farmers, women were expected to do the bulk of cultivation while men looked after the cattle.

3 Though by then, other considerations were coming into play like the greater malleability and obedience of what was coming to be called 'tribal labor.'

4 The significance of the migratory form of labor for keeping costs down in a context of gold deposits that posed production challenges is underlined by Crush, Jeeves and Yudelman: "If large numbers of low wage, unskilled workers had not been recruited from throughout the subcontinent, there would never have been a deep level gold mining industry in South Africa. The world's largest supplier of gold would have been, at best, a minor producer pecking away at the surface outcrops of enormous deep lying reefs. If a … (similar) ore body had been discovered in Australia, Canada or the United States it would almost certainly have been left in the ground because of the inability to mobilize the right kind of work force" (1991, p. 1).

Marriage would then allow him to approach the chief for his own land. So the migratory form of labor had quite complex pre-conditions.

Nevertheless, migrant labor was not a total solution to the labor problem of the mines. While it kept down the reservation wage, or the minimum that the African was willing to work for, it did not determine the level to which competition between the mines might push actual wages above it. The result was an agreement between the mines belonging to their umbrella organization, the Chamber of Mines, for it to be, in effect, a monopsonistic hirer of African labor power. In short, a wage ceiling would be imposed. However, the relatively low wage that resulted could only be effective in the context of migrant labor, since otherwise workers simply would not have shown up. It would not have provided them with enough to support their families; which is why the mines were so keen on maintaining migratory labor and limiting the permanent urbanization of the African.

But to some degree, to the extent that the mines solved their labor problems, the problem was shifted on to the backs of white farmers. Contracts with labor tenants were with the head of household and did not specify who in the household should perform the labor services. What the white landowner preferred were the younger men (Morris, 1980.) But if they were off at the mines this was not possible. And to the degree that farmers were anxious to hire wage workers, the same problem of shortage ensued. In fact, labor shortage was to be a perennial problem in the 'white' rural areas at least until the 1960s when mechanization came in and this, like the dependence of the mines on migratory labor, was to be a significant condition for entrenching the racialized institutional fix under apartheid. In particular white farmers engaged in strategies of what one might call spatial entrapment: attach the African to the individual white farm and, if that failed, to the 'white' rural areas, while removing alternative possibilities of gaining a livelihood. This was a compromise solution.

For through the grossly misnamed Natives Land Act of 1913 the more commercially minded farmers had hoped to move to a farm labor regime of exclusively wage workers. No new share cropping contracts were to be allowed and farms were to be limited to five labor tenants. But there were escape clauses, even if they were not fulfilled in their entirety. Those labor tenants who found themselves 'illegal' were to be given a reprieve till such time as land would be released for them elsewhere. The same applied to sharecroppers; they would be allowed to stay, even though 'illegal' in the sense that any new contract with the white farmer was proscribed. Again, land was supposed to be found for them, but the promises were reneged on, so they remained on the white farms.

In a situation of labor scarcity, share cropping and labor tenancy were particularly attractive to the white farmer and for many, this continued. In both instances, the African gained access to land for cultivation and livestock. The fact of crops in the ground minimized the risk that the sharecropper or labor tenant might leave before the harvest. These arrangements also appealed to Africans to some degree since they allowed them to keep the cattle essential to the institution of bride wealth or lobola.

With wage workers or what were called 'farm servants' the practice of signing the African's pass was pressed into service. For the farm servant to leave, the farmer had to sign what was called 'a trek pass.' One problem was 'desertion'[5] to the towns. This is why there was continuous agitation for stricter enforcement of the pass laws in the cities. Accordingly, from 1930 on, urban employers could be fined for taking on someone whose pass identified him as a farm employee. If the African could not be attached to a particular white farm, then trapping him in the 'white' rural areas might do the trick. Bolt holes had to be stopped up. Native reserves should, accordingly, be limited in size. This was a major reason why the original promises at the time of the 1913 Land Act to provide those labor tenants and sharecroppers who found themselves 'illegal' with alternatives in the form of land released to them were never acted on.[6]

We should enter two remarks here. The first is that these 'solutions' on the part of white farming and the mines simply tended to reproduce the fact of labor shortage. They locked white farmers and immediate producers into production relations which would postpone that revolution in agricultural productivity that could be the only permanent basis for resolving the labor shortage in South Africa. To the extent that farm workers were trapped on white farms, then the upward pressure on wages that would provide the incentive for revolutionizing productivity and so releasing workers to the mines and elsewhere, was absent. Labor tenants were primarily farming for subsistence and provided another captive labor force. And as for the reserves, they might

5 The term 'desertion' is significant signifying the severe limits to the development of a rural labor market in which immediate producers were supposed to be 'free' to search for the highest wage and best working conditions.

6 At the time of the 1913 Land Act this had brought white farming into some conflict with the mines (Lacey, 1981, Chapter 4). While the mines wanted larger reserves and the release of land for 'illegals' the white farming lobby wanted neither. For the mines it was a question of assuring the subsistence base of their (migrant) workers. Labor tenant families and sharecroppers were a source of migrant mine workers alongside those from the native reserves. Through the Native Labor Regulation Act of 1911, the farm lobby did succeed in sharply limiting the areas within which the mines could actively recruit: these were largely, though not entirely, defined by those enclaves where Africans continued to live a subsistence, largely tribal, way of life. But outside those enclaves, Africans could always move to recruitment centers in those areas where they were so allowed (Crush, 1993).

indeed provide the migratory worker with a subsistence base. But the customary tenure in force there, and still in force to the present day, inhibited the development of agricultural productivity and of an agricultural base which would effectively result in the expulsion of some Africans who would have to rely permanently on the labor market. Without private ownership there could be no credit for there was no collateral; grazing in common presented its own problems for livestock improvement; and expansion through taking over the land of others was precluded.[7]

The second point is that none of this would have been possible without the structures of the colonial state. The alternatives that Africans had were extraordinarily limited by state fiat. If they had had the vote, it beggars comprehension that they would have accepted the labor hiring rules of the Chamber of Mines with their very low wage ceiling, or the Masters and Servants laws which coerced them on white farms, and the pass laws which kept them there. The same goes for the 1913 Natives Land Act which restricted the ability of Africans to farm on their own account outside the reserves, since they were prohibited from buying land there; or even making a commercial go of it inside the reserves since the latter comprised such a small proportion of South Africa's cultivable land surface. And as we will see shortly, it seemed very unlikely at that time that the colonial state would be challenged by those who suffered at its hands.

Moreover, what was being laid down was a new institutional basis for capitalism in South Africa that would spread from the gold mines elsewhere. As we have seen, migratory labor became the labor source for the gold mines. In turn it depended to a very considerable degree on the existence of the native reserves where the subsistence base of the African miner's family could be secured. Keeping labor costs down and allowing South African gold to be competitive on the world market, and so to facilitate the flow of value throughout the South African economy came to depend on it. Under apartheid, these were to receive wider applicability and new meanings. Among other things, apartheid was an attempt to make migratory labor not just the source of choice for the mines but for all white employers – farmers, industry, the docks and the municipalities. And in addition to their role as providing means of subsistence to the miner's family, the reserves would acquire new political meanings intended to prolong white rule in South Africa.

But emphatically, what was taking shape in South Africa was inseparable from more global influences and limits. The accumulation project based on

7 Though informal rental arrangements between one land holder and another did emerge.

gold mining depended for its success on keeping costs down. It was always in a wider, more global context of mining possibilities that South African gold was judged to be expensive to mine. This was the origin of the reliance on migratory labor and the wage ceiling for Africans. But without the colonial state, that would not have been possible. Likewise when we talk about the institutional structure that had preceded the mineral revolution and that was to limit its alternatives in recruiting labor, that too had its ultimate origins in wider movements and subsequent encounters, not least that of European immigrants pushing a settlement frontier east and northeast and bringing with them, if not always practicing, the institutions of commodity exchange, and Africans, who at some time in the recent past had entered the area from further north

The construction of South Africa therefore was in the context of a meeting of capital and workers, of market institutions with those of a self-sufficient African agriculture, of a hybrid form of tenure on white farms, mixing some production for the market with forms of labor tenancy and share cropping which echoed what the indigenous population had been used to under tribal rule – the white farmer, in effect became the new chief – of technologies of force in which Europeans enjoyed a superiority, and under colonial conditions that were brought in from outside. But it was also a meeting of peoples; peoples from Europe, peoples from Africa, peoples from India and the old Dutch East Indies; people, therefore, of different phenotypes, different material expectations, all jostling together in a labor market, however imperfectly that labor market might function in some instances. The gold mines certainly drew on the racial stereotypes of the time in order to justify their practices; working in the mines, it was said, would be a way of civilizing the black man, teaching him discipline, punctuality and the superior ways of the white man.[8] But despite the interests that one might have expected workers to share when confronting employers, they also divided very clearly along lines that were racial in character. Given the widespread acceptance of ideas of racial difference at that time, ideas that the Europeans brought with them, and the pressures of the labor market, one should not have expected anything different. This was to be the source of more racial legislation, not just in the mines but elsewhere in South Africa.

3.3 *Labor's Racial Hierarchy*

At the start, gold mining depended on some skilled labor and this had to be imported. These were the white miners. They brought with them particular

8 Never the white woman! See Luli Callinicos (1982, p. 106).

views as to what was an acceptable standard of living and this determined their wage demands. But there were also African miners and their wage demands were considerably less. They had a much more modest set of claims corresponding to a relatively unsophisticated subsistence way of life in which people grew their own food, built their own shelter, wove their own garments, and saw as yet little need for state-provided public services or infrastructure like all-weather roads, hospitals and schools. This would not have been a problem if there had been no competition between them and the white miners. But technological change in the mines and learning on the job by Africans meant that eventually whites could be replaced by cheaper workers. In consequence white miners demanded job reservation. The higher paying jobs should be reserved for whites. This was cloaked in racist argument. Africans should not even be allowed to take the exam for a blaster's certificate: they were deemed too simple-minded to be able to cope with the demands of the job. Handling dangerous explosives was something with which only whites could be trusted. Or: The future of civilization in South Africa depended on providing the white man with a decent wage and so forestalling his degradation to the level of the black man. And so on.

In pressing their demands the white miners had the advantage of the vote. It was not, however, just a matter of the white miners. Whites everywhere were insecure about the labor market challenge, not only of Africans, but of Indians and Coloreds too. Further legislation was passed to ensure job reservation in other areas of the economy. This was the purpose of the tellingly termed 'civilized labor' policy from 1924 on. This mandated job reservation in anything that was state-owned including the railroads and the nascent steel industry. And when firms applied to the state for some sort of regulatory favor like tariff protection, the quid pro quo would be the introduction and enforcement of job reservation.

Indians and Coloreds had their own concerns about being undercut by Africans. Unlike the Africans they urbanized relatively early on. Wage labor forced them into the marketplace to acquire basic consumption goods; while publicly enforced standards of housing and collective provision meant an appropriate need for money to pay taxes. In the Durban area there was an informal job reservation system that extended to Indians (Freund, 1995). In the westernmost parts of the Cape, attempts on the part of Colored organizations to exclude Africans from certain jobs or even from the whole area have a long history. In fact it is fair to say that the very emergence of a Colored race group, its formation, was the result of labor market conflicts, in particular in the Cape Town area at the end of the nineteenth century (Goldin, 1987). They saw themselves as different but significantly it was not just that they looked different in virtue of their mixed-race origin, because often that was not the case. Rather they brought in all manner of cultural baggage to justify their separateness: the fact that they spoke Afrikaans, belonged to the same Dutch Reformed church as the Afrikaners, albeit separately, and were more educated than Africans. Moreover, up until the abolition of the Colored franchise in the Cape in 1956 they benefited from being able to bring their electoral power to bear on the matter. But even afterwards, they were awarded some geographical protection by apartheid governments as a sort of guilt payment.[9]

In these struggles the African working class was always at a disadvantage. This was not just because Africans lacked the vote. It was also that they were not effectively organized in order to bring to fruition the sorts of pressures that might have resulted in granting the franchise. In this regard we have to give more careful attention to their semi-proletarianized status; the fact that their separation from the means of production, notably land, was only partial, that they did enjoy such access, just not to a sufficient degree to assure their entire subsistence. It was this which made them such an easy target, not just for other fractions of the working class but for the mining industry and commercial agriculture. For the fact is, Africans were politically weak not just in virtue of the structure of the South African state, though that surely was important; but also because their social situation did not provide them with the sort of incentive framework that has always been the precondition for a strong workers' movement capable of exercising decisive pressure on the state, either in their struggles against capital or against labor aristocracies (Cox, 2004, pp. 35–39). Semi-proletarianization meant that they were not fully exposed to the social risks inherent in a capitalist economy; the risks of unemployment, of old age, of eviction from housing, of finding a job for their children. If unemployed, they could always return to the social safety net of the homestead in the reserves or even that of the family and extended kinship network on a white farm. Even if wage labor became a more insistent and even rewarding part of a life, land rights in the reserves were typically retained as security for old age. This is a hugely important fact in South African political history. As we will see, it was only as Africans became more completely proletarianized that the labor movement grew apace among African workers from the early 1970s on, and that serious pressure was exerted on the South African government. There was

9 This was the Eiselen line, drawn through Cape Province. To the west employers were required to offer positions to Coloreds before they could be awarded to Africans. As for the guilt, the view was that through their supposedly unholy behavior, Afrikaner men had been responsible for bringing the Colored race into being.

resistance to apartheid during the 1950s, but how deep its support base was, is very much open to question.

The upshot of all these developments is that from the start of the twentieth century, a racialized social structure is defined to an increasingly sharp degree. There is a white state and a white capitalist class. There is also a highly racialized stratification system owing in significant part to the effects of various job reservations: whites on top, Indians and Coloreds in the middle, and Africans on the bottom. Race seems to rule, even if underneath it all it are material concerns that are the conditioning factors: the need to keep costs down if gold is to be the basis of the South African economy; the need to limit access to the better jobs so as to achieve a modicum of (white) working class security, not to mention some self-respect in virtue of an ability to attain capitalist norms of self-reliance, property ownership, and domestic accoutrements.

This does not explain entirely the resolutely racist character of the South African state and indeed of South African society *toute entière*, and the fact that it became even more racist with the passage of time. After all, subsisting alongside the racism of colonialism had always been a competing view. Without recognition of a basic humanity shared by whites and people of color, slavery would never have been abolished.[10] In addition there was always the idea of tutelage: that under European supervision the indigenous peoples would acquire the capacities necessary to being granted the same rights and responsibilities as their teachers. This was reflected in the property character of the franchise in the Cape: all adult males who owned property to the value of at least £25 had the right to vote, regardless of race.

But clearly Cape liberalism as it was called did not survive. It was grandfathered into the South African constitution in 1910, but applied only to Africans in the Cape, where they were in fact a minority, before being abolished in 1936. One can only conjecture why this was. Prior to the discovery of gold, what had prevailed in South Africa, particularly on the advancing frontier of white settlement, was a more mercantile sort of capitalism. This was a capitalism of simple commodity producers, each owning the means of production or enjoying access to them, drawing on her own labor and entering into exchange through a merchant stratum. Equality had a material reality that it was to lose with the discovery of gold and the advent of industrial capitalism. What was crucial to the latter was not the exchange of products between producers but the creation and reproduction of labor markets as a necessary condition for making a

10 We should note here that it was abolished in the Cape in 1833, or thirty-two years before abolition in the United States.

profit. This presented a number of challenges for capital, workers and the state. These would result in the sedimentation of racial divides – a process of race formation, in other words – racist narratives and racist solutions.

In creating a labor market, all the old colonial shibboleths were pressed into service: Putting pressure on Africans to work for a wage would expose them to the civilizing ways of the white man and allow their emancipation from savagery; the native should not be pampered since that would weaken his strong constitution; and so on. White workers faced different challenges from those of white business. Theirs was the competition of African labor. They would try to cope with this by excluding them from certain occupations, again on racial grounds, but this time in terms of a racial incapacity to handle certain sorts of work. This brought them into conflict with the mine owners who were happy to bracket their racial attitudes if it meant hiring workers for less. But in a colonial state workers had a say and the government had no alternative but to take their side.

The labor problem was different for the mine owners than for the white miners, therefore. They wanted to minimize the wage bill. Converting Africans into wage workers was part of the solution but this ran afoul of white miners who feared for their own jobs. So the result was a compromise. What they could all agree on, if with some ambivalence on the part of the mine owners, was that Africans should be there to serve the needs of the white man (sic.) and not their own needs. Accordingly, successive political parties found that the race card was a sure winner. The institutional context for making money from gold mining and giving 'white' South Africa, at least, an enviable position in a global division of labor, was put in place and it was a racist one.

•••

Capitalism made modern South Africa. It was the central driving force in its creation, including its geographic definition as a 'country' and its acceptance by other 'countries' as such, not least by those, like Great Britain, that were there at its painful birth. This meant, necessarily, that it would be insertion into wider markets of capital, labor and the crucial commodity of gold that would leave a lasting mark. Things came together from a variety of places at a variety of geographic scales: the global and notably the British Empire, for sure, but also Southern Africa as a whole, as in the flows of migratory labor from outside the boundaries of what would slowly emerge as a country.

Building a country for capitalism was always, and enduringly, a matter of struggle. Creating a working class for the mines brought the dominant element of capital face to face not just with Africans who had to be 'persuaded' to work for the mines and on its terms, but also with a more skilled white stratum anxious about its privileges. Making a space for capitalism in Southern Africa also meant imposing capitalist production relations on an agrarian order where the rule of the commodity had been quite limited. This would entail a struggle between the urban and the rural which was not really settled until the 1960s, the mechanization of 'white' farming and the solution of the white farmer's labor problem.

Clearly these were struggles that, while unleashed by the development of capitalism in the sub-continent, did not occur on a tabula rasa. What was to be South Africa might have been a backwater of the global economy, such as it was in the second half of the nineteenth century, but much had happened that would create not only limits but also possibilities and not just the fact of agrarian institutions of a predominantly pre-capitalist sort. There had already been small islands of capitalist growth. The discovery of diamonds around Kimberley in 1867 had been the occasion for the development of labor practices, including the compound and migratory labor, that would later bear fruit in the much more significant gold mining industry. The answer to labor shortages in the sugar industry of Natal had been different: the introduction of large numbers of Indians as indentured workers. This would further complicate the formation of the race regime to be at the center of social life in South Africa, as indeed did the earlier introduction of slaves not just from Africa but from the Dutch East Indies. Ensconced on white farms, sex with white masters would engender phenotypical forms that could form the substrate of yet another 'race' even while the motivation for that differentiation was of a thoroughly material sort (Goldin, 1987).

What came together in what would be South Africa were people with very different geographies and experiences and not least of course, those settlers of British and Dutch origin with their distinct identities. Capitalism would bring about new interactions, new tensions and struggles and new identities as people were converted into wage workers or saw new opportunities for material enhancement in serving the needs of the gold mining industry. These would be interactions and struggles that would not be contained within the subcontinent but which would stretch overseas as South African gold assumed a key role in the globalizing tendencies of the late nineteenth century.

They would be battles, though, that would be fought in languages not confined to that of the commodity. Identities as capitalists, wage workers, simple commodity producers, or petit bourgeois would co-exist with, even be submerged by, ones of ethnicity and race, even while the underlying tensions were those entailed by the unfolding accumulation process and the all-consuming drive to ensure the expanded reproduction of capital. It would be against a backdrop of 'European' and 'non-European', Afrikaner and Brit in contrast to African, Colored, and Indian, a race consciousness taken for granted in the developed world of the time, that capital would exercise its fundamental formative role in the coming into being of a country to be called South Africa. The state would be a capitalist state, but it would also be a white one and to be 'South African' was likewise to be white; a very exclusionary conception of a country, therefore. The language of the state reflected what was happening in civil society and reinforced it by legitimating identities in formation. As capitalism penetrated into every nook and cranny of this new country and as in turn old notions of race were challenged, this would have to change but not without a strong rearguard resistance, as we will see in the next chapter.

CHAPTER 3

Apartheid and Giving New Life to 'South Africa'

1 Introduction

'South Africa' was the 'country' created to facilitate the rise of the gold mining industry in Southern Africa. It took shape in the form of a state that could ensure the institutional conditions necessary for the success of gold. In order to legitimate these institutional forms a pre-existing consciousness of racial difference, something taken for granted in metropolitan and colonial worlds alike, could be mobilized. The accommodations that had to be made with the white working class then ensured the outward racial form of the society. It looked like a settler society every bit as much as it did a capitalist one, and this was to give trouble to later attempts to understand the country.

Nevertheless, by the late 1930s these institutional forms were looking distinctly frayed. This has been widely recognized. The crisis, notable above all in the seemingly imminent breakdown of the migratory labor system that had been so important to the profits of the gold mining companies, and then the permanent urbanization of the African, would set the stage for a competition between the major (white) political parties on how to respond to it. The victorious program would be apartheid: essentially a re-clamping back into place of the institutions that had served the gold mining industry and all those dependent on it, including the South African government, so well. Just why the apartheid road rather than an alternative, somewhat less authoritarian one which was indeed broached at the time by the white opposition in the form of the United Party, is then explained in terms of the rise and appeal of Afrikaner nationalism.

This is a very South Africa-centric analysis. Apartheid certainly was a reinforcement of the institutional status quo to ensure the continuing prosperity of gold but the dilemmas to which it was a response were far from exclusively South African; nor were they exclusively to do with a crisis of urbanization, particularly that of Africans. The challenges faced by the South African government were shared with other neo-Europes, with the imperial powers and in many ways were a microcosm of much more widely experienced tensions on the world stage. On the other hand, the way South Africa had developed hitherto, including its character as one of Mamdani's (1996) bifurcated states, the fall-out from the Boer War that had allowed it to come into being in the first

 | DOI:10.1163/9789004715585_004

TABLE 5 The urbanization of Africans compared to the other race groups

	% Urban population, African	% African population, urban	% Colored population urban	% Indian population urban	% White population urban
1921	33.6	12.5	45.8	30.0	55.8
1936	35.3	17.3	53.9	66.3	65.2
1946	42.8	21.6	58.1	70.3	72.5
1951	43.5	27.2	64.7	77.5	78.4
1961	46.5	31.8	68.3	83.2	83.6

SOURCE: AFTER OGURA, 1996, TABLE 3, P. 408

place, and the failure to solve a chronic problem of labor shortage, all played into the way the overlapping crises would be met.

Apartheid would be the 'answer.' But again, to see it as uniquely South African would be in error. Apartheid was a system of rigorous spatial planning. It was certainly a highly racialized system but its underlying spatial engineering was in no way foreign to the techniques of urban and regional planning that had been taking shape during the 1930s and which were to experience their golden years after the Second World War (Parnell, 1993; Parnell and Mabin, 1995). Likewise the language of slum clearance, relocation and rehousing resonated with West European practice. Nor was this a merely superficial appropriation. Apartheid also represented a centralization of the South African state: a centralization of existing powers and the creation of new ones. Yet again, this was not exclusively a South African development. Categories like 'urban policy' were taking shape in South Africa at this time, but so too was that the case in Western Europe and North America.

2 The Context

Apartheid is usually situated with respect to an emergent urban question. Urbanization did indeed undergo a marked acceleration during the 1930s and 1940s in South Africa and it applied across all the races. What attracted concern, however, was specifically African urbanization even though Africans were still and by far the least urbanized (Table 5).

A mainstay of gold mine profitability had been migratory labor. The miner's family stayed behind, either in a native reserve or on a white farm, where they gained their means of subsistence. That meant that the reserve wage of the African miner would be substantially less than if he had been looking for money sufficient to reproduce spouse and children as well as himself. By the 1930s, though, as increasing numbers of Africans left the countryside permanently for the city, bringing their families with them or forming families in the city, the tide seemed to be turning against this particular form of low wage policy. In opposing these developments the mines could draw upon the support of other white interests. Many of the African miners came from the white farms and their permanent urbanization was aggravating a labor shortage about which white farmers had seemingly always been chronic complainers. There were also the anxieties of white workers, particularly Afrikaners, who had been driven out of the countryside as white agriculture became increasingly subordinated to market disciplines, so eliminating the small farmer, and who saw Africans as a threat in the urban labor market.

There had been similar concerns about African urbanization after the First World War. This had led to the first attempts to restrict permanent residence of workers and their families in the city. Legislation in the 1920s and 1930s stipulated that Africans not normally resident in the city had to be gainfully employed if they were to remain there. Migrant workers had to carry passes with the appropriate stamps so that monitoring of their movements could be possible. These were laws applied exclusively to Africans. Nevertheless, and despite attempts to control movement from the countryside and permanent settlement in the cities, Africans continued to come, to work, to marry and to settle down there. In part this was because African women were already there, recruited as maids by white families, even those of modest means. In part, it was because the municipalities had discretion in the vigor with which they enforced the pass laws. They had their own agenda and it was not necessarily that of the gold mining companies. To a significant degree it was one molded by the needs of a growing industrial sector. Manufacturing industry had expanded during the First World War and continued to grow afterwards. Industrial firms were not keen on restrictions on movement to cities. They wanted to keep wages down and saw creation of a pool of the unemployed in the cities as a way to do that. Lending further fuel to permanent urbanization was the fact that during the Second World War, attempts to limit that movement were suspended in order to promote the war effort. The African presence in all manner of ways became more and more evident to urban whites: using the same public spaces, demonstrating on behalf of higher wages, and notably through what was defined as 'native crime.'[1] But again, the significance of this is the way it played into the hands of the gold mines when they sought the re-imposition of limits on permanent African settlement in cities, as they eventually would.

This is certainly an important part of the story behind the coming of apartheid. But the crisis to which apartheid would be seen by some as the answer cannot be reduced to the question of permanent settlement and its direct implications for the gold mines; nor in its different components was the crisis uniquely South African. Three major points can be made here. First, South Africa shared with other neo-Europes the same crisis of urbanization. Declining farm prices during the depression bankrupted small farmers and expelled them from the countryside. In South Africa it was largely the Afrikaners who were affected by this. Then, during World War Two, urban employment expanded. This was in part a response to the needs of war production, particularly in North America and the old British Dominions, including South Africa. And in part a response to the need for import substitution as exports from Western Europe were cut off. Restrictions on African settlement in the cities were lifted and African urbanization rapidly increased. But to emphasize: This was not just a South African experience. Most notable of all was the crisis of urbanization in the US subsequent to the migration of African Americans from the Deep South to cities, mainly in the Midwest and Northeast.[2] This soared during the 1940s and 1950s, paving the way for the civil rights movement,[3] much as the tensions around urbanization in South Africa would lead to the demise of apartheid.

Second, the success of the Russian revolution, the fact of revolutionary challenge in Germany and Hungary, if ultimately abortive, hung like a great shadow over the capitalist world. The opening decade of the century had been one of growing labor militancy. The First World War reduced anxieties about the internationalization of class struggle but the Russian revolution and events like the 1926 General Strike in Great Britain, re-awakened them. The white labor movement in South Africa participated in this and by today's standards was quite extraordinarily militant and left leaning.[4] It had its own

1 Famously foregrounded by Paton in *Cry the Beloved Country*.

2 See James Gregory, *The Great Migration*: https://depts.washington.edu/moving1/black_migration.shtml. (Accessed July 7, 2024).

3 Piven and Cloward (1971) are particularly good on this.

4 "In the early decades of the 20th century no problem loomed so large as the labour problem. The scope and gravity of strikes were increasing. Industrial enterprises became concentrated in huge businesses, and those who ran them refused to make agreements which would allow trade unions to curtail their freedom; they were unwilling to share their authority. Without exception these business enterprises were hostile to the principle of collective bargaining.

political party, the South African Labour Party, which was strong enough in the Transvaal to win the 1914 provincial elections there. It may have had a racial quality to it as in the slogan behind which they marched during the 1922 Rand Revolt – 'Workers of the World, Unite and Fight, for a White South Africa' – but the bosses and a state that did their bidding rather than Africans, were seen as the fundamental problem: it was less a matter of 'Africans stealing jobs' and more one of profit-hungry mining companies bent on exploiting the worker by lowering wages. There were also movements among Africans, notably a strike in the gold mines in 1920, but the rise of the International Commercial and Workers Union in the late 1920s was a much more serious challenge. In addition, there was a significant communist presence[5] and this certainly worked to counter the more racist elements in the white labor unions.

But there was to be a backlash on a global scale. The attempt to create the nation as a counter-pole to the labor movement would be one of these.[6] As the international economy deteriorated during the late 1920s and early 1930s this would assume more aggressive forms, culminating in fascism and dreams of a redistribution of the world's wealth through territorial expansion: a struggle that became identified as one between the so-called 'Have Countries' – the old imperial powers, particularly Great Britain and France – and the 'Have-Nots', like Germany, Italy and Japan. South Africa would slot into these developments but, as we will see, in a distinctive way.

Finally, there was the anti-colonial movement. This would take off with vigor after the Second World War, but it was already evident in the 1920s and 1930s. In India it was sufficiently strong to give the British serious concerns during the Second World War. There had been nationalist revolts in French Indo-China. In South Africa the International Commercial Workers Union had had a distinct anti-colonial flavor in the rural areas, calling for the return of land to Africans. Calls for national independence would become much more vigorous later, but the signs were already there.

Skilled workers, who needed three years of apprenticeship, and more of practice to train, became the minority, overwhelmed by specialized unskilled workers who could be underpaid" (Visser, 2001, p. 1).

5 Again, one is reminded of how various forces and influences came together in South Africa to make it what it was and would be. The South African Communist Party was always non-racial, but much of the impetus for its formation came from the immigration at round about the turn of the century of Jews from Russia's Baltic states – the so-called Litvaks – among whom were a number profoundly schooled in revolutionary understandings. This influence was to continue through the anti-apartheid struggle right down to the present day. This is an important story that merits a more detailed study.

6 See, for example, Michael Mann (1995).

All these dilemmas and challenges were evident in South Africa: an urbanization crisis; a challenge from labor movements, if racially divided; and the anti-colonial movement. Yet their expression in South Africa was, as elsewhere, highly particularized. This meant that their resolution would necessarily take on a similarly particularized form. For a start, the implications of the permanent settlement of Africans in the cities cannot be understood except in the context of chronic labor shortage. One of the reasons for resort to the migratory labor form and then the monopsonistic hiring practices of the Chamber of Mines had been a scarcity of wage labor; this is because to have relied on the forces of the market would have resulted in a wage that would have been for the mining companies outside the bounds of making profits. White agriculture, it will be recalled, also experienced severe labor shortages, which accounts for its attempts to attach workers through share cropping and labor tenancy. By the 1930s, a new factor was coming into play. This was the increasing employment being offered by industry, typically at wages greatly in excess of those in mining and more attractive than the returns in kind to Africans on white farms. Not only that, industry was a less oppressive work experience. Accordingly, both the mines and white agriculture wanted a sharp stiffening of controls over the movement of Africans. For the mines it was a question of what would be called 'influx control': limiting the ability of workers to come and work in the cities. If 'influx' could be controlled, then it would be easier for the mines to recruit in the native reserves. For white agriculture it was a matter of what would be called 'efflux control': controlling the movement of Africans out of white rural areas. There was some tension between the mines and white agriculture and there always had been, but both could unite in opposition to the demands from industry for a relaxation rather than a stiffening of controls. The failure to more thoroughly proletarianize the African by restricting access to the land, was an important condition for the seeming intractability of the impact of permanent African urbanization on labor market conditions.

The rise of the anti-colonial movement was another challenge as in the increasing difficulties that the West European powers were facing in their colonies; a challenge that would become more severe in the post-war years. Again South Africa was far from unaffected. But the colonial problem there, was not a relation between countries; rather colonialism was internal to South Africa. Colonialism was a relation between the South African government and the hegemonic economic forces conditioning its actions, and the various spaces within which Africans reproduced themselves for work in 'white' South Africa: notably the native townships as they were called and the native reserves; or, one could argue, between the settlers and the colonized wherever they were in South Africa. In any case the colonial question was one which South Africa would have to confront within its own boundaries, either bringing the colonized into the country in a more than geographical sense: giving them political rights above all, and equality in social provision; or essentially, as the apartheid governments would do, expelling them to what were intended to be their own 'countries.' The latter would be the homeland project. From the South African government's point of view, Africans would indeed throw off South Africa's yoke just as Indians would the British, and the Indonesians the Dutch. But this could only be on white settler terms, and to be accomplished by fragmenting one country into several: a white South Africa alongside the former native reserves, each elevated into a supposedly independent homeland.

Colonial struggle was internal to South Africa *per necesita*. But, and oddly, national struggle would also be internal. During the 1930s, the Germans, the Italians and the Japanese saw themselves as engaged in a struggle for an increased share of world trade and the global product that, short of a formal re-division of empire between them and the Haves, would have to be achieved by force. In South Africa the confrontation was between the Afrikaner nationalist movement on the one side and the English-speaking whites on the other.

The mass appeal of Afrikaner nationalism was material. It certainly exploited the sense of historic hurt at the hands of the British; notably the Boer War and the loss of independence of the Afrikaner republics. But what was really at issue was the ongoing fact that Afrikaners were the low people on the white totem pole. The Afrikaner business class was poorly developed and among the workers, it was typically the English-speaking whites who held the most desirable positions. In addition, among whites, Afrikaners bore the brunt of the misery of the 1930s. So support for the National Party, the party of Afrikaner nationalism, essentially took the form of what one might call a cross-class alliance: working class Afrikaners coming together with Afrikaner business behind an agenda that would elevate them to the same level as the English speaking or beyond (O'Meara, 1983) – in other words, a movement of mass economic uplift.

•••

This is the background to the crucial election of 1948; the election in which the party of Afrikaner nationalism, the National Party, would be elected into office behind a program of what it called 'apartheid'; something whose contours were as yet vague and ill-defined, but which definitely meant more stringent limits on the urbanization of Africans. In this way the National Party hoped to appeal to the anxieties of urban whites around job market competition and the question of native crime. At the same time, it would further the interests of the Afrikaner farmers – and most white farmers were Afrikaners – by helping pin down Africans in the 'white' rural areas. This would also help the gold mines, though interestingly the anti-big business leanings of Afrikaner nationalism meant that this was not of great interest to the National Party. Still, the gold mines supported restrictions on the permanent urbanization of Africans. National Party rule would work to their advantage.

This agenda was contested. The party that had been in power since the mid-1930s, the United Party, found its support base largely among English-speaking whites. Materially more secure, they were less in favor of the sorts of restrictions on Africans being proposed by the National Party. Significantly this position had the support of industry which had been growing rapidly since the Second World War. The big concern there was that restrictions on the movement of Africans would severely challenge their labor needs. They were happy to see Africans coming freely to the cities, since that would keep wages down (Morris, 1977); the prospect of an industrial reserve army was the glint in their eyes.

In the event, the National Party's victory was a narrow one. Indeed, without the serious malapportionment that had been built into the 1910 constitution as an attempt to provide it with legitimacy among Afrikaners,[7] the United Party would have won the election. The consequences were to be momentous and the more important ones unforeseeable. What were foreseeable were indeed the improved material prospects of Afrikaners. There was to be a leveling of material outcomes, though less at the expense of the English-speaking whites than through the intensified exploitation of the African that would be one of apartheid's major effects. But by, in effect, strengthening the position of gold relative to industry in the country's economic base, apartheid governments would essentially make it much more difficult in the future to shift to a position in the international division of labor more favorable to the masses.[8] Gold, and later other minerals, locked South Africa into a set of social consequences – low skills and low incomes for the vast majority – that would make the shift to industry much more difficult. For whites it worked, but for the majority of the population, Africans in particular, it not only destroyed present lives, but it compromised future ones as well. It would make it much, much more difficult

7 Rural areas, which were dominantly Afrikaner, had been purposely divided into constituencies with smaller electorates. As a result, the rural population, which was for the most part more Afrikaner than English-speaking white, tended to be overrepresented, and became even more so with the drift to the towns.

8 This position had been reinforced by the discovery of new gold deposits in the Western Transvaal and the Orange Free State in the late 1940s.

for any post-apartheid government to fulfill its emancipatory goals; but apartheid was meant to last.

3 Apartheid

Exactly what apartheid would mean was initially unclear and it was contested. The argument broke down into two opposing positions: total apartheid versus practical apartheid (Posel, 1991, pp. 49–60; Lazar, 1993). Total apartheid was an extremely radical move in the direction of resolving the colonial question: taking apartheid or separate development seriously, therefore, by a disentangling of economic relations and giving Africans their independence. This was to be achieved through several related steps. All Africans would be consigned to the reserves and these would eventually become independent states; the exact boundaries of these states were left undecided and there was talk of massive economic assistance from the South African government to facilitate their development.[9] At the same time the economic integration of white and black that had been occurring in the cities of South Africa – largely a matter of white employers and black employees – would be rapidly reversed. Black workers would be replaced by a mix of machines and of immigrants from Europe, primarily from the displaced persons' camps that were a residue of the Second World War. The result would be a purely white South Africa and the elimination of that dependence on black labor which might result in claims for the vote.

But this resolution did not sit well with capital. Inevitably there were concerns over labor supply. To replace blacks with machinery would be extremely expensive. The success of any immigration drive was uncertain. Capital's preference was for a watered-down version of 'total' apartheid; something more 'practical.' Yet it was far from united on what form this 'practical' sense should take, and this returned the National Party to the arguments that had preceded the 1948 election. In that campaign Smuts's United Party had argued for a more relaxed approach to the permanent settlement of Africans in the city. The belief was that it was inevitable and difficult to control. This had sat well with manufacturing industry. They wanted a more settled labor force and they wanted that industrial reserve army that uncontrolled African movement to the cities would virtually guarantee. On the other hand, and as we have seen, mining and commercial agriculture strongly disagreed. Mining wanted

9 This leaves the Coloreds and the Indians out of the picture. For the Coloreds, a Colored homeland, presumably to achieve independence, was proposed. The Indians would eventually be repatriated to India.

the reproduction of the migrant labor system and agriculture wanted control over the movement of workers from the 'white' rural areas. In the event, of course, the result was a compromise, and within that compromise, room to address the interests of the three main contenders for African labor.

Over the long-term total apartheid would be the goal, but over the short term it was 'impractical.' There would be steps in the direction of total apartheid, but at the same time, labor supplies would be protected. The outcome was more one for mining and commercial agriculture, but there would also be some consideration of the requirements of manufacturing. There was some hedging of bets, therefore, but only 'some' and certainly not enough to offset the growing tendencies to 'lock-in' in the South African economy: an extractive future rather than a stronger emphasis on manufacturing. More concretely, the major features of the 'solution' that emerged included the following:

1. Influx control: Through resort once more to passes[10] and a system of labor bureaux, the permanent African presence in the city would be subject to stringent regulation, even curtailed. Increasingly the only terms on which Africans could work in the city would be as migrant workers. They would not be allowed to bring other, non-working members of their families with them. A system that had originally developed to answer the labor needs of the gold mines was now to be extended more rigorously to other sectors of the urban economy. A rider to this legislation was a concession to white farmers, designed to protect their labor supply. While the 'white' rural areas would also be served by labor bureaux through which city jobs could be secured by Africans, the actual take-up of jobs would be conditional on approval by a local committee on which white farmers would sit. This was known as efflux control.

2. 'Section Tenners': So-called 'Section Tenners' were those Africans given permanent urban residence rights. The idea here was to cater to those needs of industry for skilled workers that migrant workers could not satisfy. This was particularly important in the country's industrial center of gravity, stretching from Pretoria in the north, through the Rand to the Vaal Triangle in the south:[11] particularly important since, unlike Cape Town or Durban, there was no intermediate layer of, respectively, Coloreds and Indians to assume that role. The term 'Section Tenner' was a reference to a clause, Section Ten, in the Bantu (Urban Areas) Consolidation Act of 1946, which had actually been enacted by Smuts's United Party government; an early attempt, therefore, to

10 These were personal identity documents and more, for they could include details of the holder's work history, along with various official stamps indicating the 'urban rights' he or she might have.

11 The Vaal Triangle was an area bounded by Vereeniging, Vanderbijlpark and Sasolburg.

respond to concerns about the increasing urbanization of Africans, but one whose detailed enforcement was left up to individual municipalities. Section Ten laid out the rules governing exactly who could be given permanent urban residence rights.[12] The National Party implemented other policies designed to build up this skilled African working class. These included the introduction for the first time of state schools for Africans,[13] the construction of hospitals and a vastly extended housing construction program. This might seem a step away from the ultimate goal of 'total' apartheid. But the temporary sojourner status that the government was anxious to impose on all urban Africans was underlined by a proscription of homeownership; something which could be justified legally by reference to the land ownership provisions of the 1913 Land Act. At the same time there were attempts to counter the detribalization that went along with permanent – or at least, as far as the apartheid authorities were concerned, quasi-permanent – urban residence. This was through segregation by tribe in the allocation of housing in the townships.

3. Homelands: The 1913 legislation had declared certain very limited areas of South Africa off limits to white ownership. These were the native reserves. They were hugely important as areas of origin of migrant workers for the country's urban employers, including the mines, as we have seen. The plan of the National Party, not immediately apparent but slowly emergent, was to build them up, firstly as self-governing; and then to award them full independence. There was some plausibility to this project. Not least there was a degree of cultural differentiation among the populations of the different reserves, primarily along linguistic lines. In some cases, notably the Zulus, a 'national' history could be constructed. Tribes were to be converted into nations. Ultimately all Africans could look forward to 'repatriation', whether they lived in the cities or in the 'white' rural areas.

In short, South Africa was to be the arena for some audacious social engineering, a massive project in urban and regional planning, and Africans were its object. They were to be relocated, reorganized, given new subjectivities, and their physical movements limited. The tendencies had already been apparent before apartheid: the attempts, that is, to control influx, to remove Africans from more racially desegregated housing conditions and to place them in their own 'locations.' But this was far more stentorian and ambitious. Parts of

12 For example: Birth in the city; continuous employment by the same employer for ten years.

13 This was the so-called, Bantu education, much reviled by the liberation movement for its second-rate, even tribalizing character, but as Hyslop (1993) argues, for many African parents it had its advantages.

this scheme were, as we will see, carried out. Others proved more difficult. In particular, migrant labor continued on a massive, even increasing, scale. The colonial form of the South African state endured but from the standpoint of people of color, particularly Africans, the suffering was intense and has been well-documented (Platzky and Walker, 1985).

It was, furthermore, an ongoing program. Total apartheid remained a distant if somewhat fuzzy objective, and constantly shifting in its details, often in response to very pragmatic concerns. The proposal to transform the native reserves into independent homelands was undoubtedly brought forward in time. This was a result of the internal resistance from Africans to the raft of apartheid legislation which followed the National Party victory in 1948; and external pressures originating in the growing anti-racial and anti-colonial mood developing among the major world powers of the time. The homeland project was seen as a way of relieving these pressures. Africans would indeed get the vote that they had been pressing for, the right to determine their own futures; it was just that it would not be in a (rump) South Africa.

Independent homelands opened up new prospects of pursuing the apartheid dream, perhaps even achieving that total apartheid which had been postponed in the early years. During the 1960s the government expended a major effort to end the labor shortages of the 'white' rural areas once and for all. This would be through a government-subsidized program of mechanization, drastically cutting down on the need for African labor and liberating the most traditional of white farmers from reliance on the ox teams of their – still in evidence – sharecroppers. The question was: What to do with the Africans who had lived and worked on white-owned farms? The answer was 'resettlement': a bundle of forced relocations aimed, according to the ruling apartheid ideology, at uniting Africans with their 'ethnic brothers and sisters' in the homelands (see Figure 2).[14,15] What this meant, in effect, was confinement to what were essentially rural slums: desolate settlements like Glenmore in the Ciskei and Loskop in KwaZulu, where people had no access to land, no access to employment in the immediate vicinity and a future, if such it could be called, that was

14 The same fate awaited the residents of what came to be known as 'black spots.' These were areas of African peasant colonization outside the reserves in those areas that, in the 1913 legislation, had been declared off limits to African land ownership. Their establishment had preceded the Land Act and they were grandfathered in. They consisted of privately owned farms and were the outcome of African purchase, often collective, of white farms. Many of them had been purchased in anticipation of the 1913 Land Act. Under apartheid, however, and with the same project of 'whitening the platteland' in mind, they had to go, and for the most part, they did.

15 The definitive text on 'resettlement' is Platzky and Walker (1985).

limited to long distance commuting or migrant labor. More importantly, the separation of Africans from the land was now well and truly underway, and apartheid policies were centrally implicated in this; an audacious act of ethnic cleansing that was to bear bitter fruit for the apartheid authorities in the years to come.

Pushing in the same direction of attaching Africans to the homelands and reducing their presence in 'white' South Africa were various measures introduced in the 1960s. These included steps to locate new African townships destined to serve major cities, in adjacent homelands, where this was geographically possible; and a concerted attempt to disperse industrial employment from the major urban centers of the country to locations within commuting distance of settlements in the homelands and later to so-called 'growth points' in the homelands themselves.

One of the dilemmas of controlling the African presence in the cities had to do with an increase in the number of Section Tenners: those with permanent urban residence rights. This was not so much a matter of unanticipated yet

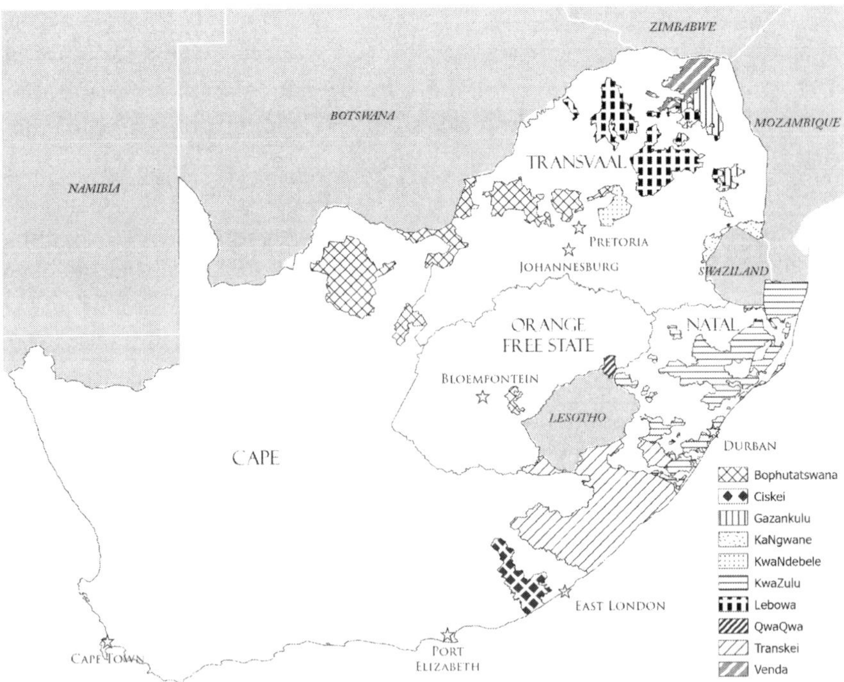

FIGURE 2 The South African Homelands
MAP BY RUIXUAN DING. SHAPE FILES KINDLY MADE AVAILABLE BY BRENT MCCUSKER

successful applications for Section Ten status as it was simply one of population increase. The children of Section Tenners acquired the same status, and as they got married they looked for housing. But by offering them formal housing in new townships in adjacent homeland locations, this presence could not only be controlled; it also gave the government an opportunity: new formal housing would come with the dubious prize of citizenship in a homeland and so the forfeiture of Section Ten rights.

Employment dispersion had a different origin. The fact was that influx control in the 1950s was only a qualified success. If anything, the numbers of Africans in the cities as migrant workers grew. This was partly due to employer preferences. Under the influx control legislation any new jobs in the city were supposed to be offered to Section Tenners through a labor bureau system. Only when that proved fruitless could migrant workers be recruited through labor bureaux in the homelands. But inevitably Africans made their way to the city outside this system of controls, and employers took them on. For many tasks migrant workers were preferred on account of those same 'tribal' features that had been attractive to the mining industry. In any case, illegals were common. In some of the homelands land hunger was biting hard and the risk was worth it, for the chance of being endorsed out of the city could be reduced to some degree. Africans developed all manner of micro-resistances to exploit the evident difficulties of monitoring the African presence in the city. Passbook inspections were particularly likely in certain places and at certain times – like train station exits at rush hour – and Africans learnt how to avoid them.

In short, the early evidence was that the influx control machinery was not working as well as had been desired. There was a view that the local governments were far too complicit with local employers in the way that they managed respective labor bureaux, conniving in their frequent preference for migrant workers. This led in 1971 to their replacement by Administration Boards, comprising, territorially, numerous contiguous local governments. Officials were appointed by, and immediately responsible to, the national government (Posel, 1991, Chapter 9).

Stopping up the loopholes was one approach. Relocating employment was then seen as a major way of keeping Africans in the homelands and away from the 'white' cities. Limits were placed on the numbers of Africans that could be employed there. This was typically in the form of a ratio of African to white workers that had to be observed by employers if additional Africans were to be taken on. Alongside this stick were the carrots of subsidies and new physical infrastructure in the form of industrial estates for relocation to points close to the homelands from which Africans could commute on a daily basis.

The net effect of these different policies, varied in the logics informing them, was a quite massive change in African geography. The proportion of the African population living in the homelands increased dramatically. 'Resettlement', the location of new African townships to serve white cities, the new possibilities of commuting to jobs just over the homeland border, all worked their various effects. In 1960 the proportion of Africans living in what were to be the homelands was 39%; by 1983 it was a startling 54%. Likewise, while Africans had always been the least urbanized of the four population groups, their urbanization had now been reversed.

This was not the case with the Coloreds and the Indians. They remained outside this web of controls and forced relocations and were not, therefore, subject to influx control. By the time of apartheid, they were already significantly urbanized and there was no migrant labor rationale for keeping them out. How they were affected by apartheid was through the Group Areas Act and the purposeful attempts of successive governments to provide them with an intermediate position in the racial hierarchy.

The Group Areas Act was an early piece of apartheid legislation, and one that rightly added to its notoriety. It envisaged the division of the city into racially exclusive residential areas for whites, Coloreds and Indians. Africans were to be catered for in townships, typically on the urban periphery or even located at some geographic remove. Africans were affected by it, since in many cases they were located in areas defined for exclusively white, Colored or Indian use; but Coloreds and Indians bore the brunt with District Six, the Colored neighborhood in Cape Town, and Cato Manor, an Indian area in Durban, the iconic instances.[16]

On the other hand, as with the construction of the African townships, there was also a slum clearance element to the program, inspired by post-war European visions of urban planning. Bill Freund (1995, p. 72) noted how many Indians in the Durban area had lacked basic amenities like mains water and electricity, so affordable, publicly owned, housing, if racially segregated, had some appeal. It also meant an end to exploitation and rack renting in the slum areas on the part of Indian landlords. So, the effect of the Act on Indians, at least, was a mixed one.

Quite where the inspiration for Group Areas came from is unclear. It was certainly in accordance with the National Party's ideology of separateness, but we have seen that there were typically material interests behind other aspects

16 Note should also be taken of the forced and highly contested removal of Africans from Sophiatown, an African freehold neighborhood in Johannesburg that had been grandfathered in by the provisions of the 1913 Land Act.

of apartheid legislation as well. There were white pressures for vigorous residential segregation. There had been local legislation in Durban towards achieving this goal. There were more general concerns on the part of Afrikaner small shopkeepers to contain the stiff competition that Indians offered, particularly in the small towns of the Transvaal; confining Indian retailers to an Indian Group Area defined so as to remove them from the central business district was certainly part of the agenda. But why separate Indians from Coloreds, except to maintain consistency with some ideologically inspired blueprint?

Even so, Coloreds and Indians were to be treated differently from Africans. Group Areas legislation applied to the permanently urbanized population while the status of Africans was more ambivalent; so while Section Ten status seemed to confer permanent rights of urban residence, quite how 'permanent' was never made clear. Rather there was also a tendency to treat any African in the city as what was called 'a temporary sojourner.' Accordingly, while Coloreds and Indians could own property Africans could not; rather any formal housing they lived in was owned by the municipality.[17]

Coloreds and Indians were seen as answering certain needs in the urban division of labor, particularly for more skilled workers. This worked in Cape Town and in Durban, but elsewhere, as in Johannesburg, Port Elizabeth and Pretoria, and as remarked above, Section Tenners were supposed to function in the same way. So, and as I have tried to emphasize, there was a material vision behind apartheid legislation and the various controls it placed on Africans, Coloreds and Indians respectively.

This summary of apartheid on the ground is to emphasize the material. For many observers the notion of 'separate development' or apartheid was a highly racialized program. This needs to be qualified. At the discursive level changes were occurring that would later factor into efforts to construct a coalition of forces of a multi-racial sort so as to defend apartheid. During the period from the 1920s through to 1948 that institutionally goes under the heading 'segregation', the major division of the population in white thinking was between Non-Europeans or Natives[18] and Europeans. Natives were regarded relatively homogeneously and, despite the fact of separate Afrikaner and English-speaking white identities, so were Europeans; certainly more so than they were to become. The dominant way in which the relation between European and native was imagined was racial, drawing on all those dualisms of an egregious

17 And this, of course, could be justified in terms of the 1913 Land Act and its proscriptions on African land ownership outside of the native reserves.

18 'Non-European' was the more expansive term since, in addition to Africans, it included Coloreds and Indians.

sort that concluded with the need for white dominance in the affairs of state and business. The rise of Afrikaner nationalism in the 1930s, however, initially in the form of the Purified National Party, was to change this. This is because it's emphasis on a distinct Afrikaner identity, an Afrikaner nation, opened up tensions with simple racial taxonomies; something that was never to be resolved under forty-two years of governments pushing and defending an apartheid agenda.[19]

For the National Party that won the crucial election of 1948 injected a national taxonomy into the way in which difference was to be subsequently thought in South Africa. This in turn entailed the introduction of ideas of shared ethnicity and the significance of shared beliefs and culture: something at odds with the, hitherto, dominantly racial way of thinking about difference. Part of this clearly came from the way in which Afrikaners were invited to distinguish themselves from English-speaking whites.

'Separate development' would seek justification for itself by a similar appeal to culture and ethnicity. For what were to be 'separately developed' were the Bantu nations; with the execution of the homeland project from the early 1960s on, these assumed center stage. Colored and Indian development was also to be separate and to be provided for, as in the creation of their own universities: the University of the Western Cape for Coloreds, and Durban-Westville University for Indians, though, intriguingly, faculty were often white. Later, separate development was to be further embellished with ideas of equal freedoms, multi-nationalism and, still further down the road, that of power sharing between constituent 'nations' or 'groups.'

It is certainly the case that some of this change corresponded to a shift in Afrikaner thinking as successive governments faced very practical challenges. We have already seen how the idea of homelands was quickly wheeled out in response to the changing political situation as decolonization got under way in the rest of Africa. Yet from the very start, there was a co-presence of racialization and ethnicization, hierarchy and difference, oppression and self-determination. This was certainly a source of division within the National Party and those thinkers who provided it with its ideological justifications. Practical apartheid inevitably lent itself to more racialized understandings than total apartheid. Similarly, the decision in 1983 to create a tri-cameral legislature in which Coloreds and Indians, alongside whites, would elect their own representatives to respective legislative chambers was hotly contested. It led to

19 On these issues, Aletta Norval (1996) is particularly informative.

the breakaway of a very significant number of National Party MPs to form the Conservative Party.

This is by no means to give the imaginary and the discursive formation of identities an autonomy with respect to the material changes that were occurring in South Africa. The breakaway of the National Party's extreme right to form the Conservative Party in 1982 corresponded in significant part to a class division (Charney, 1984). Moreover, the embrace of the national and of national difference, while it might seem to represent a shift away from racial understandings, could also be turned against the movement for a non-racial franchise within South Africa, as indeed it was in the form of the homeland project.

This of course leaves the white working class out of the picture. They too were implicated in the apartheid project, if not always in intended ways and not just in terms of the Afrikaner-Brit divide. Above all, the super-exploitation of Africans set in motion by apartheid allowed an integration of white workers into the state, regardless of whether they were Afrikaner or English speaking, on a much larger scale and finally putting paid to any serious threat to capital's hegemony. This is an integration that assumes a quantum leap with the mass economic uplift of Afrikaners. Mining revenues continued to expand well into the 1970s, providing the basis for an expansion of state and industrial employment, both. The white domestic market grew rapidly creating a seemingly virtuous circle between consumption and industrial growth: what Stephen Gelb (1987) has referred to as racial Fordism. Foreign investment expanded noticeably, particularly during the 1960s and subsequent to the successful stifling of the resistance of the 1950s.

As elsewhere in the advanced capitalist world, these were boom times; what has been referred to as the Golden Age of capitalism. Increasing fractions of the white working class in the advanced industrial societies found themselves in a position to buy the first family car, owner occupancy increased, people moved into the suburbs and into white collar jobs. No wonder they felt that they had moved up in the world and there was talk in the US of an enduring Republican majority and in Britain, to paraphrase the title of an influential book of the late 1950s, the question was raised 'Must Labour Lose?'[20] The old battle cries of the first two decades of the century seemed increasingly irrelevant.

The Cold War completed the rout. Socialism was not quite yet a dirty word, but the construction of communism as an evil, uneven as the process was, further eroded the more radical wing of the labor movement and helped pave the

20 As in the book of the same title (1960) by Mark Abrams, Richard Rose, and Rita Hiden.

way for the reformist right, particularly in its party political incarnation, to take over and assume control: a project that had been in the works since at least the 1920s when the electoral threat of the left first became evident.

4 An Assessment

The racial hierarchy that apartheid governments constructed was an extraordinarily rigid one. There were clear tendencies in that direction prior to 1948[21] but apartheid would substantially bolster the view that South Africa was utterly exceptional, and not in any flattering sense. Even so, it is a case that does not elude the grasp of more generalized understandings. Again one returns to the logic of accumulation and how accumulation is driven by the forces of class struggle. Class struggle is something that all capitalist states must contend with. It generates tensions at the point of production which the state must then handle if the social formation of which it is the (self-interested) carapace is to endure. Policies have to be devised, rhetorics fashioned, that will defuse and co-opt, even while the vitality of the accumulation process remains unimpaired. There is, in short, a problem of state legitimacy that is universal across all capitalist societies.

To some degree the working class itself can provide a field of opportunities for the state to exploit. The fact is, the working class everywhere exhibits highly contradictory tendencies. On the one hand there are moves towards working class unity – a drive to expand working class rights, including the right to the vote and social rights via the welfare state and labor law. Unions engage in unionization battles with employers as they seek to expand their membership. Working class parties are formed, sometimes financed by the union movement.

21 Compare Denoon and Nyeko (1987): "many of the nationalist government's measures of the 1950s merely put the finishing touches to machinery which already existed. Racially mixed marriages were banned – but interracial sexuality had already been prohibited by the Immorality Act of 1927. The Population Registration machinery of the 1950s merely made it more difficult for individuals to sneak across the barriers of race which already existed. The provision of different syllabi for African school children (and then the provision of separate universities for different races in the late 1950s) took to a logical conclusion the actual segregation which already prevailed in almost every school in the country. The disenfranchisement of Coloreds followed logically from the earlier removal of Africans to separate electoral rolls and representation. All of these measures were implicit in the 1910 constitution, and in the interaction of political forces represented by that document" (p. 69).

Organization occurs across national boundaries, albeit more weakly than within.

Just as clearly there are tendencies to fragmentation. The development of the technical division of labor provides a material condition for this: a division into better paying, more secure positions, and ones that are less well paid and more subject to instability. Those with the technical capacities to occupy the more attractive positions seek to monopolize access to them in order to limit the competition that would drive down salaries and wages and make their jobs less secure and even relegate them to those regarded, in capital's scale of values, as less worthy. Credentialization works in this direction, but paradoxically the union movement itself can become another vehicle. Minimum wages and conditions of work favor the more skilled against the competition of the less so, since from an employer's viewpoint, the latter are seen as less productive and so vulnerable to the possibility of displacement by machinery. But insecurity is never far away, and attempts to maintain a monopoly of the better paid jobs a constant, working itself out in all manner of ways: recruitment through kin and acquaintance networks, a neighborhood segregation that can play into differences in formal education, and then justified in terms of stigmatized difference deriving from all manner of personal histories: religion, immigrant status, an origin in the 'backward' rural areas, language and, of course, phenotype.

Difference aside, this stratification creates obvious possibilities for capital. Not the least of these is an electoral alliance with the more privileged strata of the working class, which is how the party politics of capitalist democracies tends to work anyway. Where the working class develops its own political parties, there is the possibility for the right of working with the less threatening elements around some vision of the 'national' interest, perhaps through a coalition government in which a party of the left is inducted into 'how to govern.' In this way capital's rule can be legitimated, but only by a redefinition of what is 'inside' and what is 'outside' the state, or what is 'inside' and 'outside' a cross-party consensus. To the extent that the excluded challenge this particular fix, this then becomes problematic to capital and to the state, and the dialectic is repeated. New groups have to be integrated into the national consensus, if only through those ideological blandishments that Marx's famous 'freedom, equality, property and Bentham' make possible.

In South Africa the fragmenting tendencies in the working class were particularly strong. The struggle around job reservation that climaxed in the Rand revolt of 1922 suggests that this was conditional, at least in part, on significant differences in the value of labor power and the threat that Africans in particular posed for white workers once they had acquired the necessary competencies and could handle more technically demanding work.[22] However, given the form of the colonial state, and its racial franchise, white labor market anxieties could then be, and in fact were, translated into enduring labor market protections: job reservation, and advantages with respect to access for formal education; something that would become increasingly important as the division of labor became more complex. The stability of these arrangements varied. This could work for a while, given limits on the proletarianization of Africans. The fact that most still enjoyed some access to land, either on a white farm or in the native reserves, meant that issues of wages and job security were less pressing than in the case of Europeans. Moreover, contracts were entered into with no idea when the experience might be repeated; so pressing for improved wages and conditions of work might yield results of marginal benefit. But once the migratory labor system began to break down, Africans started organizing to protect their interests in the city both as workers and as residents, and it became problematic. Accordingly, the miners' strike of 1946 and the Sofosonke movement of shack dwellers (Bonner, 1991), both focused on the Rand, generated serious anxiety for the political class. The threat of African political mobilization was very clearly 'in the air', as Paton's Cry the Beloved Country demonstrated.

The response of the white ruling class in its efforts to create a stable coalition of forces, was to be what was known as grand apartheid. Africans would indeed get the vote but not in South Africa; rather it would be in their own states or what were called 'homelands.' The state, in other words, would instigate limits to the integration of the South African working class by externalizing the vast proportion of its African component. Influx control measures and the so-called 'whitening of the platteland' and the forced relocation of Africans to the reserves were part of this policy. Despite clear government intentionality, the absence of any organic evolution in the emergence of homelands as political objects, and the resultant widespread cynicism on the part of the African liberation movement, this just might have worked but the conditions were ones that the South African government was unwilling to implement.

---

22 With respect to differences in the value of labor power one is reminded of Marx's claim regarding the use values entering into its determination: "the number and extent of his so-called necessary requirements, as also the manner in which they are satisfied, are themselves products of history, and depend therefore to a great extent on the level of civilization attained by a country; in particular they depend on the habits and expectations with which the class of free workers has been formed" (1867; republished 1976, p. 275). On the Rand in South Africa this would certainly have differed between, on the one hand, recent immigrants from Europe and on the other, Africans from a rural subsistence background.

For the most part, and from the very start, the homelands lacked an economic base. White farming interests, largely Afrikaner and therefore an important element in the social base of the National Party, limited the territorial expansion of the reserves, which might just have allowed the expansion of commercial farming. The report of the Tomlinson Commission of 1954 favored measures that would have made the homelands more economically viable. It called for a massive program of government investment in order to build up the physical infrastructure and provide a basis for industrial development. It also recommended tenure reform, notably the replacement of tribal tenure by private property, so as to promote agrarian change and the development of productivity on the land. The first recommendation ran afoul of white business interests in South Africa. Their concern was that any serious industrial development in the homelands would have negative consequences for the flow of migratory labor; something significant for their profitability, particularly for the mines. And as far as the abolition of tribal tenure was concerned, the anxieties were those of the South African government and complemented those of the mines. For if migratory labor was to continue then everything should be done to consolidate the rule of the chiefs and the durability of the tribe since it was believed that African political quiescence depended on them.

•••

One of the more positive effects of the interest in globalization has been to point towards a new way of understanding the specificity of particular places. It did this by sensitizing to the importance of placing countries in wider contexts of influences and conditions. South Africa is very specific indeed but that does not mean to say that it is to be understood in terms of relations and conditions entirely contained within it; that what was constructed there was constructed on the basis of conditions found only there. Rather, what was unique was the juxtaposition of forces and conditions that came together from diverse locations throughout the world at the southernmost tip of the African continent and which then both enabled and constrained the creation of a particular institutional fix for capitalist development. Processes of race formation, the racialized institutions through which class tensions were expressed, make no sense outside of the extension into the area of the structures of colonialism, the pressures of the world market and the encounter between Europeans and so-called 'indigenous' peoples; 'so-called' because in a world of flows and movements and periodic sedimentations, nothing is irreducibly indigenous. Everything came and continues to come from somewhere else to encounter other conditions elsewhere and to be transformed into something that it was not.

South Africa was always a work in progress. More accurately perhaps in terms of what was happening elsewhere in the world, it should be called a work in retrogression. A racialized form of social relations was there from the start and it both deepened and widened over time. Apartheid is often thought of as a sharp break in the country's history but that can easily be challenged. Again, it is too easy to ascribe the particular changes brought about by apartheid to forces seemingly internal to South Africa, like the rise of Afrikaner nationalism. Afrikaners contrasted what they believed to be their own stronger African roots with the divided loyalties of the English-speaking whites, so the Afrikaner nationalist frame of reference was always with respect to a field of relations extending outside the country. During the Second World War there was a strand of opinion in the Afrikaner nationalist community that hoped for a German victory, and they certainly opposed South African involvement in the war. The belief was that a German victory over the British would mean that Afrikaners might then regain freedom in their own country once more. For the Afrikaner the British were always the resented imperial masters even though South African was independent from 1910 on.

The global frame of reference for apartheid, however, was more extensive still. In a sense the Brit / Afrikaner struggle was just the fluff on the surface. Much more central to the post-World War II debate was the future of an accumulation project out of which virtually all whites, regardless of language and cultural affiliation had done relatively well; certainly far better than those who they defined as 'non-Europeans.' Poverty is always relative and while there were indeed poor Afrikaners their poverty was nothing compared to that of the black masses, whether African, Colored or Indian. But by the end of the Second World War it was clear that the institutional basis of that accumulation project was no longer as secure as it had once seemed. Apartheid aimed to renew it and give white supremacy a new lease of life, which it did.

South Africa was molded in the context of influences of a more global character, therefore, and it is in terms of those influences that its peculiarities are to be understood. But by the same token, those peculiarities shed light on the global. Just what has been and remains possible under conditions of capitalist globalization and how those possibilities are converted into actual social forms never ceases to amaze and many times, horrify. The constraints, the anxieties, the contradictions, the conflicts are manifestly social, and people try to deal with them through all the resources, social, technological, political, cultural, and geographic, at their disposal. These are emphatically resources of a social nature, available like the metaphorical Ritz, to all, but access to which is always mediated by money. As social resources they are necessarily geographic; people relate to them over space, and over the last five hundred years space has increasingly meant the global. But they always relate unequally. So the solutions are inevitably for some and not for all. There are always material stratifications and moral hierarchies and they tend to map onto each other.

If the horrifying has been possible, so too has been the emancipatory. The capitalism which underpins global trajectories gave birth to labor movements. These in turn have succeeded in improving the material standards of working classes and in a political emancipation, if always on capital's terms. Capitalist development is a contradictory process, generating pressures which it cannot help but generate and which it would rather do without. Once again, the pressures and the emancipatory possibilities are social and therefore increasingly global in character.

For a while apartheid was perfectly adequate as a solution to the dilemmas confronting South African business in the immediate postwar period. There were, however, changes afoot and apartheid governments could not control them. Not least they could not control the rise of the anti-racial and anti-colonial movement in the rest of the world; something that came to matter more and more with the development of political institutions at the global level and of a worldwide anti-racist discourse, and inseparable from the internationalization of the labor movement and its discourse. Its response to this was the creation of the homelands and a concomitant ethnic cleansing. This, however, and obviously inadvertently, meant that apartheid governments were digging their own grave. More global struggles about the future of capitalism in the form of the Cold War gave them a breathing space but when those struggles were seemingly resolved, the game was up. It is to that particular story that we must now turn.

CHAPTER 4

In the Eye of the Storm and the End of the Beginning

1 Introduction

The history of apartheid can be divided very roughly into two periods. The first, from the election of a National Party government in 1948 up until the early 1970s is one in which as a policy, and from the standpoint of its protagonists, it enjoys no small measure of success. There was certainly opposition on the part of Africans, Coloreds and Indians, though how deep the forces of organized resistance were, how much popular support they had, has been put in some doubt,[1] and by 1960 the opposition had been crushed. The African National Congress and the South African Communist Party had both been banned. International opposition was still in its infancy. The National Party had consolidated its electoral dominance in the country. What would follow would be a decade of unprecedented growth. Foreign investment entered the country with a vengeance as American corporations established branch plants alongside those previously set up by the British.

1973 represents a turning point. This is the year of the Durban dock strike, largely African, in which the quiescence of the 1960s was seemingly shattered and, given the way in which it spread to other parts of the local economy, in dramatic fashion. But it was emphatically symbolic. Through the sheer spontaneity of the event, the fact that there was no union leadership since the government did not recognize African labor unions, it suggested some new, latent power among Africans; a power born of their increasing proletarianization. It also coincided with increasing difficulties in the global economy; difficulties that would have major implications for the future of apartheid.

From the early 1970s on, the National Party is struggling to adapt to circumstances, and not just those of a global economy whose prospects were clearly less promising. In addition, the anti-colonial movement becomes a much more serious challenge. Southern Africa emerges as a cockpit of the struggle. By 1980

1 "While African political leaders from the very beginning demanded rights of political representation within the national state, it was not until the late 1970s that generalized demands for political inclusion could be said to have animated a broad cross-section of the black population as a whole" (Ashforth, 1997, p. 104).

 DOI:10.1163/9789004715585_005

all the neighboring states, Angola, Botswana, the former Southern Rhodesia and Mozambique are independent of colonial rule, and with African-majority governments willing to assist the forces of African resistance in South Africa. South Africa had become the odd country out and hence the focus of an anti-colonial struggle whose energy had been hitherto diffused over a wider front.

Finally, there is 'globalization.' This covers a number of different developments. Deterioration in world economic conditions after the early 1970s results in a search for a way out, a way back to the corporate profitability of the so-called 'golden years' of the previous two decades. 'Globalization' is, in the first place, the nice ideological cover invented to represent what is actually a neo-liberal 'solution' to the problem. It takes some time to emerge but by the 1980s its lineaments are clear. Liberating finance on a global scale, the elimination of capital controls, subordinating national currencies to short term financial movements, will subordinate labor to the rule of capital and rein in what were seen as its unreasonable pretensions. The market will rule and the state will withdraw; de-regulation will be the order of the day; none of which sounds particularly compatible with the highly regulated society that South Africa had become, though as we will see this represented less a problem and more an opportunity for a government which by then was looking for a way out of its deepening dilemmas. Yet the meanings of globalization are multiple and can in no way be confined to the economic. Among other things, it meant cheaper air travel, e-mail, the internet, a global media industry, all of which would have important cultural effects in South Africa, and especially among the white population. In quite complex ways, none of them would work in favor of apartheid's survival.

This is the background to the changing balance of political forces in South Africa. Very broadly two things happened. On the one hand, those outside the South African state – both within South Africa itself and without – brought unprecedented pressure on it on behalf of inclusion; and on the other, the reasons for continued exclusion of people of color lost their force. Apartheid no longer seemed a necessary evil in the changed circumstances of the world; malign but not necessary.

As far as the anti-apartheid movement was concerned one can identify three distinct components, sometimes combining, sometimes not, from the mid-1970s on. The first is the rise of the African labor movement. The Durban dock strike was evidence of a newfound strength but African labor unions are not recognized by the government until 1979. From then on the growth of membership is, without exaggeration, remarkable (Bhorat, Naidoo and Yu, 2014). The second is the rise of urban African youth, for the most part high school students, who became the shock troops of the anti-apartheid movement. If the

1973 Durban dock strike was a big surprise for the government, so too was the Soweto uprising of 1976. Students would continue to be a thorn in the side of the government and would play the lead role in the more generalized township revolt of 1984–86. Finally, there is the so-called civic movement which gathers strength from 1982 onwards. The initial reason for the formation of civic groups was opposition to the Constitution Act of 1983, an act which sought to divide the opposition forces by granting limited democratic rights to Asians and Coloreds but not to Africans. They then became active in boycotts that set in around increased rents, service charges and public transport fares as the government sought to confront a fiscal crisis brought about by the deterioration in the global economy.

On the other hand, and lending its own weight to the changing balance of political forces in South Africa, support for the continuation of apartheid declined. From the mid-1980s on South African capital was clearly looking for a way out of the crisis gripping the country. The investment climate had deteriorated. There were anxieties about the possibility of international sanctions as the anti-apartheid movement in North America and in the United Kingdom grew in strength. There were difficulties investing overseas. Most of the rest of Africa was off-limits; an area that was in a sense natural for the expansion of South African corporations given some familiarity with African conditions and its relative proximity. The same applied to much of the rest of the world as a result of sanctions imposed on takeovers by companies registered in South Africa.[2] By the end of the 80s feelers were being made to ANC representatives.

Among the white population as a whole there was also some loss of support. For many whites the labor market threat to their incomes subsequent to a putative dissolution of apartheid was no longer there. They had the experience and credentials to shelter them from competition. There was also an increased willingness to move overseas if, under any new regime, it should be warranted. Support for apartheid was becoming more and more lukewarm, even tepid, and confined to the poorer strata and what remained of the fierce Afrikaner nationalism of the 1940s and 1950s. Their home from 1983 on was the Conservative Party, but they were never able to mount a serious challenge to a National Party that started out trying to reform apartheid in the late 1970s and ended up by deciding to scrap it. The white working class would be hung out to dry, the most desperate elements finding themselves living in the sort of shanty towns that they had thought more appropriate to Africans.

2 Though there were ways round this. See Hattingh (2007).

In all of these developments, the changing global forces and conditions outlined earlier were all in play in some way. The South Africa government tried to respond to these, but often in ways which merely aggravated the situation and served to undermine its defense of apartheid. It could not have known how its actions would play out and what forces it would unleash. We now turn to these global developments and how they were implicated in the shifting balance of political forces either individually or in combination with one another: a changing balance which would result in the overthrow of the particular institutional fix that was apartheid.

2 From the Golden Years to the Long Downturn

In the conclusions to his book *Forty Lost Years* (1996, pp. 472–478), on the rise and fall of apartheid, Dan O'Meara is keen to underline the significance of the wider, global political economy. During the Bretton Woods era, lasting from the immediate post-war years to the early 1970s, relatively rapid rates of growth in the world economy facilitated the apartheid project. Apartheid was a brake on the accumulation process but money could be made anyway. With the breakdown of the Bretton Woods settlement and the advent of what would come to be called 'globalization', the global economy entered a phase much more adverse to capital anywhere in the world and this increased the tensions between apartheid and South African business; tensions which would be an important part of the background to its dissolution. Although one might disagree with the details of his argument, in particular the way he frames it in terms of state autonomy and its rise and fall, his instincts are surely correct. One cannot make sense of the way apartheid was able to thrive and then to dissolve without taking into account developments in the global economy. The post-war upswing, the so-called 'golden years' followed by the 'long downturn' (Brenner, 1998) from the early 1970s on are absolutely crucial to what happened.

Apartheid was not a cheap project. Influx control, the homelands, the policing of the black masses, the duplication of bureaucracies for the different race groups, all cost money. Given the available statistics, in order to demonstrate that the apartheid state was a top-heavy one in terms of the size of its public service, is not easy. Nevertheless, it may be significant that between 1950 and 1970 it expanded by 129% and between 1950 and 1980 by a quite massive 232%.[3] The various items of racial legislation also had an effect on the accumulation

3 Naidoo (2005, Table 5.1, p. 114).

process, particularly in industry. Wage costs were inflated through the distortions introduced into the labor market by job reservation and influx control (Moll, 1991). Towards the end of the apartheid era, the shortage of appropriate labor skills became a major issue for industrial employers. There again, the spatial organization of society imposed by apartheid introduced inefficiencies that the government tried to make good through subsidies. Urban geography was quite perverse: jobs at the center and those least able to afford the commute, living on the periphery. So, the government subsidized transportation. But government revenues to pay for these had to come from somewhere.

At the start none of this was of great moment. This was not just a matter of the fact that initial resistance was weak, but the longer apartheid lasted, the greater it was, and the more money the government had to plough into countering that resistance, and seducing through spending – like increasing the money spent on black schools. Rather during the early years, economic conditions at the global level were extraordinarily propitious to the sort of expensive social engineering that was apartheid. As indicated above, the period from about 1950 to about 1973–74 corresponds to what some have called 'the golden age of capitalism'; years of rapid expansion in the global economy, buoyant demand for commodities and labor, and, more to the point, increasing state revenues. Under such favorable conditions, expensive state projects like apartheid were not the deadweight on the national economy that they were later to become.

Table 6 shows what happened. Figures refer to annual rates of increase by decade of gross domestic product per person: a crude measure of increasing output per person and therefore of increasing wealth. The pattern is clear. Before 1970 rates of growth are quite high and in the case of Germany and Japan, spectacular. After 1970 there are very considerable declines. Even today, the rates of growth attained in that early period have, with few exceptions, yet to be approached. South Africa shared in this pattern (Table 6), though at considerably lower rates of growth. Its collapse has been particularly brutal (Figure 3). Even so, we should note that over the period 1950 to 1970, and taking compound interest into account, gross domestic product per person increased by almost fifty percent. In other words, in its early years apartheid experienced quite favorable economic circumstances.

The long downturn worked against it, particularly given the challenges of the anti-colonial movement. It was during this period that apartheid began to be threatened on both domestic and international fronts. State expenditures on the internal security forces, on various forms of spending to shore up

TABLE 6 Average annual rates of increase in GDP per capita by decade.

	1950–1960	1960–1970	1970–1980	1980–1990	1990–2000
France	4.32	5.46	2.95	2.01	1.76
Germany	9.85	4.07	2.82	1.29	1.92
UK	2.59	2.45	2.01	2.71	2.27
Western Europe	5.16	4.41	2.83	2.00	1.91
US	1.85	3.27	2.36	2.49	2.24
Japan	10.75	14.37	3.82	4.00	1.20
South Africa	2.00	2.94	0.85	-1.25	0.35

SOURCE: 1950 DATA: HTTPS://WWW.NATIONMASTER.COM/COUNTRY-INFO/STATS/ECONOMY/GDP-PER-CAPITA-IN-1950. (ACCESSED JULY 7, 2024). 1960 DATA: HTTPS://DATA.WORLDBANK.ORG/INDICATOR/NY.GDP.PCAP.KD.ZG. (ACCESSED JULY 7, 2024)

the defensive ramparts of apartheid, had to rise accordingly.[4] Not least, South Africa found itself surrounded by a set of hostile states willing to give succor to the South African resistance movement. These were the so-called 'front-line states.' Dealing with this cost money: money to support opposition movements there that would make life uncomfortable for governments, and also to support a relatively large military establishment to defend borders from guerilla incursions. Moreover, the South African military included many highly skilled whites who would otherwise have been employed in the private economy.

Part of the fallout of the long downturn for capitalist societies was the fiscal crisis of the state. At the end of the 1970s this was something keenly felt. On the one hand, demands on governments were increasing; on the other, as a result of the relative decline in economic activity, revenues were lagging. Raising taxes and government service charges was one option, but this carried risks of popular disapproval. In some ways the fiscal crisis confronting the South African state in its relations with urban Africans was particularly severe. This

4 In 1960 military spending as a percent of total government expenditure stood at 3.2%; five years later it was 7.4%. By 1978 it reached 18% and never went below 10% thereafter. See Batchelor, Dunne and Lamb (2002).

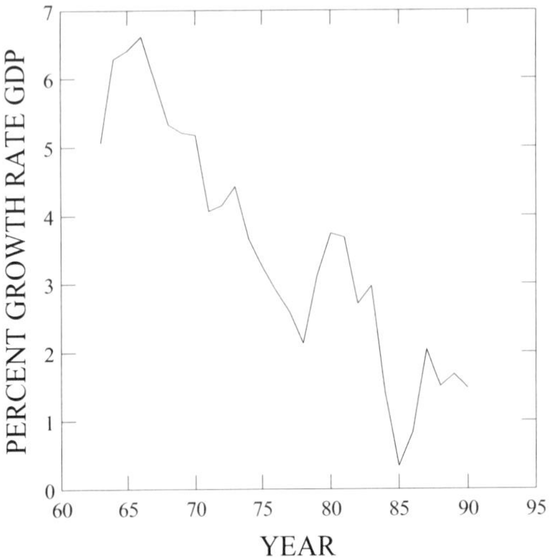

FIGURE 3 Changes in GDP growth in South Africa: 5-year moving mean. Note that this is GDP and not GDP per capita: hence figures that are more flattering than those in Table 6
SOURCE: HTTPS://WWW.MACROTRENDS.NET/GLOBAL-METRICS/COUNTRIES/ZAF/SOUTH-AFRICA/GDP-GROWTH-RATE#:~:TEXT=IT%20IS%20CALCULATED%20WITHOUT%20MAKING,8.73%25. (ACCESSED JULY 8, 2024)

was because of its role not just as tax collector and public service provider, but also, since virtually all township housing was government owned, the government happened to be the rent collector. Raising rents was an attractive option for reducing its arrears, but again there was a risk. The government was very exposed.

What it then sought to do, in effect, was distance itself from the process by devolving responsibility for large areas of public provision to newly established black municipalities. Hitherto urban Africans had been governed by branches of the central state known as Administration Boards. They were the ones who allocated housing, provided services and collected rents and service charges. From 1982 on, this would be the responsibility of Africans themselves. In this way the central government tried to shield itself from black anger at its shortcomings by, in a sense, making Africans responsible for Africans, but without state subsidy. The risk in doing this must surely have been calculated, but it was also seen as a move to assuage the demand of urban Africans for a voice in the way they were governed. Henceforth, they would elect black councilors.

The tactic backfired badly. But in order to fully understand why that was, one must also recognize how government policy was affected by the impending decline of gold as a fundamental element in the country's economic base. At the time of the National Party's coming to power in 1948, industry had struggled to make its voice heard. National Party policies of regulating the allocation of African labor through influx and efflux control worked to the advantage of the mines and white agriculture but were a problem for industry. It was not just that influx control tended to entail labor turnover in a context where competitive capacities often meant a protracted learning on the job. It was also that influx control, admitting Africans to urban labor markets only if they already had a job, worked against industry's preference for a pool of unemployed in the city ready to respond to sudden increases in labor demand, and to act as a drag on the wages of the remainder when demand slackened (Morris, 1977).

Nevertheless, during the 1960s industrial employment surged, particularly in the wake of the investments of foreign corporations anxious to tap a growing domestic market, notably among whites. On top of that, gold production peaked in 1970 and it began to be appreciated in policy circles that the days when the country could rely on it as the basis of its major role in the international division of labor were limited. South Africa would have to produce more of its industrial goods itself so that it did not have to rely on gold exports to pay for its imports of manufactures and / or export them so that it could continue to import those beyond its technical capacity.

It was with this in mind that the government embarked on an ambitious program of improving the education of urban African youth. The goal was to help ameliorate the supply of skilled workers for industry. A massive expansion of secondary education and technical training followed, starting in the early 1970s. That this policy enjoyed some success is evident in the increasing numbers of urban Africans in clerical and technical positions.[5] The problem was that, on the one hand, this increase of those in secondary education was an increase of those Africans most likely to be politicized. And on the other, the fact that the resources allocated to the process were inadequate, so that classrooms were overcrowded and teachers poorly prepared, increased the likelihood that they would indeed be politicized (Hyslop, 1988).

5 The absolute numbers of Africans in routine white-collar employment had been increasing since 1965 (Crankshaw, 1996, Figure 5). What is more interesting is the clear inflection point in the increase in numbers of Africans, both absolutely and relatively, after the late 1970s (ibid, Figure 7).

It is with these changes in government policy as background that one can begin to appreciate some of the elements of sharpened resistance to the regime. Students had already made their presence felt at the time of the Soweto riots in 1976 and would continue to do so in the 1980s through their orchestration of school boycotts and worker stayaways. From the early 1980s onwards, and in the wake of the creation of the black municipalities and their policies, the government would also have to contend with more middle-class African resistance. This was in the form of the civics or citizen organizations. They made their first appearance in the popular resistance to the Constitution Act of 1983: a piece of legislation that gave Coloreds and Indians some democratic representation at the national level, albeit in their own legislative chambers, but none to Africans.

Urban Africans were supposed to be happy with the new black municipalities, but they were little short of disastrous and quickly drew the wrath of residents. Housing was henceforth to be a municipal responsibility. Expansion and maintenance of the housing stock would be up to them, and without any subsidy from the central government. Rents would have to cover their needs, even though, as the urban African population had expanded through natural increase, there was a considerable backlog in supply. A response to the housing shortage on the part of those directly suffering from it was the construction of informal housing. It was also a way of avoiding paying higher rents. So the black municipalities not only raised rents; they also demolished informal housing. One possibility of fiscal mitigation was what quickly became known as 'development': the improvement and leasing of land for white owned supermarket chains or for the new black businesses that the government now wanted to encourage. This, however, invited corruption on the part of councilors – a significant precursor of the current situation – and so intensified the popular opprobrium. Adding further to this were increased service charges. From the early 1980s the government, as part of its policy of widening industry's domestic market, embarked on a policy of electrifying the townships but this had to be paid for by the residents, regardless of their typically low incomes.

Initially it was the civics that spearheaded the resistance through rent strikes and refusal to pay increased service charges. Urban youth then joined in. Black councilors were violently attacked, and black police stations likewise. The government intervened with force, students were arrested, which give them an additional reason for calling school boycotts and worker stayaways.

The general effect was to heighten awareness of the lack of political rights.[6] There was the strong sense that the state was not listening to local demands.

The civics did not always appreciate the violence of the students. What they shared though was their education, and their education could, as pointed out above, be traced back to policies that the South African government had implemented in order to confront a growing economic crisis. Educating urban Africans would be the answer. But what it produced was on the one hand a stratum of white-collar workers, nurses, teachers, and technical workers, articulate and knowledgeable, and able to take on leadership of civic organizations. And on the other, through the botched way in which the new educational policies were implemented, a mass of urban youth whose aspirations had been raised but left unsatisfied.

3 'Globalization'

The answer to the crisis of capitalism that was the long downturn would be 'globalization.' First came the fiscal crisis of the state; and second the news that it was a mistake for states to have been so ambitious in the first place – that nothing could substitute for the market, and what is more, the market on a global scale. If states had subordinated themselves to the rule of the market then things would have worked out fine. But as currencies were allowed to float, as capital controls were abolished and trade liberalized, and markets encroached on what had been state territory, so states could absolve themselves of responsibility.

The implications for the crisis in South Africa would be mixed, except that whether the government liked it or not, apartheid for various reasons, could no longer be in its future. On the one hand, the changing nature of global economic structures, practices and discourse would limit the policy instruments at their disposal in seeking space for policies over and above the fiscal constraints that they were confronting; they would also integrate banks into new international practices that would ultimately expose the South African economy to severe shocks. On the other, through claims about de-regulation and privatization and neoliberal strategies more generally, the new discourse of globalization would facilitate some dismantling of apartheid. Even a transition to a non-racial democracy was being forced into consideration. And this would

6 Compare Seekings (1988): "as residents responded to grievances by organizing themselves, and the state responded to protests with overtly political repression, the initially localized grievances were seen to be bound up with the fundamental issue of access to formal political power, both locally and nationally" (p. 70).

be something about which the white middle class of South Africa was increasingly indifferent. In a variety of different ways 'globalization' was reworking their subjectivities, eroding their attachment to the white South Africa that the National Party had wanted to encourage; but also making them more willing to leave South Africa if the occasion should demand, and so less likely to dig in their heels.

Just how 'globalization' became the mantra of governments and of the financial press need not detain us. Exactly what it implied, though, is important. It was thoroughly in place by the early 80s, more in some countries like Great Britain and the US and less elsewhere, like France. But it had effects everywhere in the capitalist world and, as we will see, beyond. What was not so clear at the beginning, but which should be emphasized, was its neo-liberal character. This was a globalization that had little time for state intervention. What it meant in effect was the rule of the market and on as wide a geographic scale as possible. Its ultimate goal, however, was to restore profitability through a radical re-working of class relations.

Fundamental in making this possible was the move away from fixed exchange rates that occurred in the 1970s. Foreign exchange controls were eliminated so as to allow the new global market in national currencies to function more effectively. This paved the way for a new policy regime in which macroeconomic policy would be subject to financial flows on a global scale. This had several effects. One was to give macro-economic policy a much more austere character than hitherto. Expansionary tendencies were seen as risking inflation and so threatening the value of the national currency as wealth holders sought 'safer' currencies. Inflation might be a way out of chronic balance of payments problems as a national government sought a more realistic value but it was also risky. While it tended to lower the prices of exports and so should give a fillip to foreign exchange earnings, there would inevitably be a delay as firms moved to establish themselves in foreign markets, create new distribution networks, and expand to respond to the new demand. On the other hand, the effect of inflation was to increase import prices. Once again, building up the national production capacity in order to substitute for imports was not instantaneous. Instead of easing the balance of payments deficit, therefore, devaluation of the currency through increasing the money supply might simply make a bad situation worse as it once again became the target of speculators. So curbing the inflation rate became a major macro-economic policy target.

This constraint shifted government attention away from macro- to microeconomic policy. Instead of a devalued currency as the answer to balance-of-payments problems, firms had to become more cost efficient. This would be the basis for a further shift away from state intervention. Through floating currencies, states had entered into competition one with another in order to attract those investments, long and short term, that would buoy the national currency. The same would happen to production. The new focus would be a withdrawal of the state from production and from regulating the private market. Publicly owned industries providing inputs to private firms would be privatized in order, it was thought, to make them more competitive. Myriad state regulations of private markets would be revoked or scaled down so as to allow firms to lower their costs and become more effective competitors in international markets. There would be, in other words, a return to the verities of the market. This was the beginning of a neoliberal phase in national and international economic policy.

Meanwhile deregulation was extended to the labor market. National wage bargaining mechanisms were displaced to the plant level. Labor law was reworked in order to shift the balance of advantage to capital. The new macroeconomic goal was fighting inflation; maintaining full employment was history. The resultant austerity put pressure on workers to comply with the new dispensation. As unemployment increased, so job markets became much less worker friendly. Firms threatened closure or relocation unless contracts were renegotiated. Domestic austerity shifted attention to export markets, which gave government and business an additional justification for re-working labor law; without it, export markets would be lost. And all of this could be explained away by reference to global markets beyond the control of individual governments.

The struggle in South Africa was deeply affected by these developments. It is no accident that the township revolt of 1984–1985 corresponds to a downturn in the South African economy that was subsequent to a sharp decline in the price of gold: a downturn that the South African government could do little about unless it wanted to risk a more severe devaluation of the rand than was occurring already. This in turn was to contribute to what was, in retrospect, a decisive moment in preparing the ground for the dissolution of apartheid: the financial crisis of 1985.

Contributing to it was the way in which the internationalization of finance that accompanied the new global policy regime opened up further possibilities for financing business in South Africa. By 1985 South African investment needs had become very dependent on loans from foreign banks. This would have been inconceivable under the old Bretton Woods arrangements where there were severe limits on international lending. But by the mid-1980s things had changed very considerably. Financial transactions of all sorts, both long term direct investment and short-term loans, surged during the 1970s. In the

South African case, though, foreign investments were heavily loaded towards short term loans to South African banks. South African banks would then loan that money out long-term as part of the core finance of South African firms, always under the assumption that, as in the past, foreign banks would roll over the loans they had made. But in 1985 this suddenly changed. The South African government had tried to put an end to the township revolt by declaring a state of emergency. This sounded alarm bells in international money markets. All of a sudden the risk attached to the future of the South African economy underwent a serious deterioration and so too, therefore, did any lending to firms. Foreign banks refused to roll over existing lines of credit, resulting in economic crisis: a collapse of stock prices on the Johannesburg stock exchange, and a major run on the rand. The unwillingness of the South African government to contemplate further reform deepened the crisis and opened up cracks in the unity hitherto shown with South African business. It focused attention in a way that the township revolts had not been able to and would be a major turning point in the transition away from apartheid and towards African majority rule. Even so, the effects of 1985 were as symbolic as they were material. The decline in the value of the rand as the South African economy continued to deteriorate, had started quite a bit earlier (Figure 4).

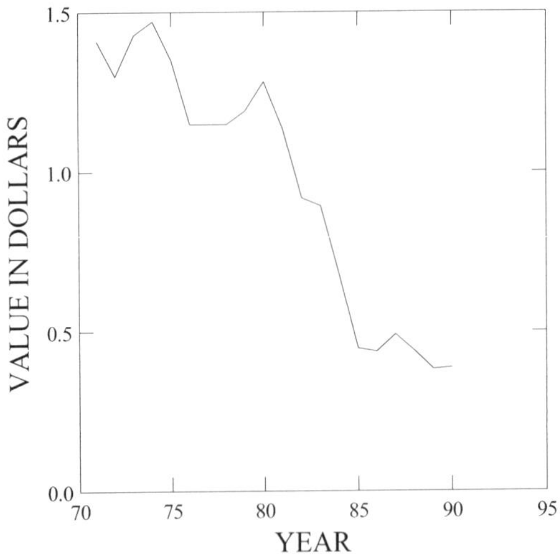

FIGURE 4 The changing value of the South African Rand
SOURCE: HTTP://WWW.ROLLINGALPHA.COM/RAND-WEAKENED-SINCE-1971/ (ACCESSED JULY 8, 2024)

On the other hand, and importantly, the neoliberal policies that were becoming so significant discursively, and then practically in those of the Reagan and Thatcher governments, also resonated in South Africa. As elsewhere apartheid governments turned to micro-economic policies as a means of confronting the decline in profitability and the need to defend the balance of payments not by devaluation, though that also happened, but through a shift away from state ownership and regulation to giving a greater play to market forces. This brought them face to face with some of the sacred cows of apartheid, not least job reservation and influx control. Both would go: job reservation in 1982 and influx control in 1986. One can interpret these moves cynically, as a way of finessing a tricky situation with the white masses where the government felt it necessary to offer signs of reform in order to draw the sting of the anti-apartheid movement. There were, though, other neoliberal moves that work counter to that sort of interpretation. Later in the decade there would be plans – but nothing more – to privatize so-called parastatal corporations like the electricity company ESKOM and the iron and steel company ISCOR. It seems that the South African government was increasingly convinced that the forms of government intervention represented by apartheid were incompatible with the new global recipes for re-booting stagnant economies. Once again, South Africa, like other countries, was being re-made by circumstances beyond its control.

In trying to understand that re-making, Simon Clarke, in an article in 1990, included South Africa in a more general understanding of the transformations that occurred in the last quarter of the twentieth century: firstly the way in which social democracy in Western Europe and, to a lesser degree, in North America, was overtaken by neoliberalism; and then how, later, the more authoritarian regimes of the Soviet Bloc and also South Africa, dismantled their, by definition, highly interventionist states. He tries to accommodate all these changes to a larger model of change in class relations on a global scale. In the case of Western Europe and North America the transformation stemmed from a political impasse between capital and labor in the context of the long downturn. This impasse created a crisis of state legitimacy.[7] This was resolved by the state absolving itself of its responsibilities, and so allowing a restructuring of class relations through the adoption of neoliberal policies and subordination to the law of value on a global scale. In a way that Notermans (1997) has then described, capital's money form was imposed on the state. This transition was achieved fairly easily in democracies where initial stages of restructuring were engaged by social democratic parties: by the Democrats under

7 Claus Offe's book, *Contradictions of the Welfare State* (1984) is very good on this.

the Carter presidency in the US, by the Callaghan Labour government in the British instance, and by the Socialist Party in France under François Mitterand. This was important to carrying out the exercise since it limited opposition by exploiting government links to the organized working class. One can add to Clarke's proposals that while in South Africa there was a similar impasse, exemplified by black resistance and the increasing concerns of capital, particularly after 1985, the breakthrough to a neoliberal resolution was not initially possible since the overwhelming proportion of the working classes had no political representation. Breaking working-class resistance required a transition to African-majority rule. Once that was accomplished then the neoliberal way was open to resolving the South African crisis; but that would be to anticipate the discussion of the next chapter.

This was all the more necessary as the South African government's white support base was increasingly lukewarm to its project. Subjectivities were changing and in a way which made them more willing to accept 'reform' of apartheid or even its abandonment. Again, globalization and what was essentially a neo-liberalization of the person, was implicated, as Jonathan Hyslop (2000) has pointed out. On the other hand, the displacement of Afrikaner solidarity by material interest, by consumerism and a hedonism that sat ill with the stern puritanism of the Dutch Reformed Church, had been underway for some time, spurred on by the arrival of television. Suspecting its potential for subversion of the received wisdom, apartheid governments had long kept it out. But from 1976 the ban was lifted, and this opened the door to English-language programming from elsewhere, most notably North America, portraying lifestyles sharply at odds with the stiff authoritarianism of white South Africa, as it then was, but lifestyles for which an increasingly wealthy and consumption-driven middle class was ready. Hyslop makes particular reference to the Cosby Show, which featured a middle-class African American family, the Huxtables, integrated into the white world of New York. But the point is, an increasingly wealthy white middle class was ready for these images of a consumption driven, sometimes hedonistic, society and equally ready to dispatch to the past the moral strictures of traditional Afrikanerdom.

There were other forces at work, forces that in a sense had been anticipated by the Afrikaner literary movement of the 1960s, known as the Sestigers:[8] a group of writers who discovered another world in France and particularly in Paris; a literary world of global dimensions to which they wanted to relate their own national traditions of writing, and often finishing up by jettisoning them. This exposure to an outside world would then continue with the cheapening

8 I am grateful to Jeff McCarthy for pointing this out.

of international travel and white South Africans discovered new worlds that were not so obviously ruled by racial dictates and which seemed to function perfectly well anyway. The declining real costs of international air travel and later, the digital revolution of long distance communication would then make escape, if it should be necessary, if the ending of apartheid threatened their middle class comforts, all the more feasible.

4 Confronting Decolonization

Decolonizing South Africa remained a problem right to the very end. No understanding of how the curtain finally dropped can possibly overlook the context provided by the anti-colonial struggle. This is widely recognized, but usually from a South African viewpoint and, furthermore, a relatively politicized one that downplays the significance of the class relations I tried to highlight in the previous section. The decolonization of the rest of Africa is typically acknowledged along with what it meant for the struggle in South Africa, particularly through the havens provided for the ANC by the so-called, and newly independent, frontline states. Likewise, there were the arguments and debates in the United Nations and attempts to censure South Africa for denial of human rights to the majority of its citizens: a discourse which the more developed countries found increasingly difficult to ignore as decolonization proceeded around the world, and so producing an increasing number of members which had once been colonies. Connections are also made to the Cold War and how the US and Western European countries were happy to overlook the oppressions of apartheid to the extent that it meant pushing back the limits of communism and providing a Western bastion of strength in an Africa dominated by formerly colonial countries, many of which had sympathies with the communist bloc. This, however, fails to adequately grasp the way in which South Africa was situated with respect to a wider, more global political economy in which, regardless of decolonization in the formal sense, colonial relations would necessarily continue in a new form: in other words, the way in which developments in South Africa were constituted by what was happening in the rest of the world, and particularly in the form of class relations.

We should start out by recalling the significance of empire for the capitalisms of North America and Western Europe. Empire was part of the expansion of the capitalist world; one of the ways in which it confronted its contradictions, developed new markets and sources of raw-materials, and discovered cultivars – tropical fruits, fibers like rubber, mild narcotics like tea and coffee and even stronger ones, like tobacco – which could be the basis of new products. This required, in turn, the creation of a physical and social infrastructure, extending in some cases to the dispossession of native[9] peoples, the creation of labor markets and of labor law. But once resistance to colonial rule set in, the problem was to ensure that, subsequent to imperial handover, a government would be left in place that was capital-friendly, that would honor its debts, refrain from nationalizing the property of Europeans and Americans, so that the extension of the capitalist world made possible by empire would remain an enduring one.

With the rise of the USSR and the eventual formation of a so-called 'communist bloc' anxieties would be heightened. The Cold War would cast a long shadow over the process of decolonization as the two major blocs conflicted over alternative geographies of capitalism and socialism; a conflict that, as a result of a newfound aggressiveness in a Republican administration in the US, would rise to a climax in the 1980s, exactly at the same time as the pressures on the South African government were intensifying. The communist bloc was a threat to the capitalist grip on a post-colonial world. It strengthened anti-colonial forces everywhere, in part through its discourse of human emancipation and anti-imperialism, in part through the training of cadres, and in part through the provision of material aid.

We should also note the geographically uneven nature of the process of decolonization. Imperial countries varied in the speed at which they yielded to the demands of independence movements. In some cases like Algeria and Kenya, the presence of settlers complicated matters. This delay was particularly evident in Southern Africa: Portugal did not let go of its colonies of Angola and Mozambique until its fascist dictatorship was overthrown in 1974; independence came the following year. Angola and Mozambique[10] also had some European settlement as did Southern Rhodesia and Namibia.[11] Southern Rhodesia would not become independent in a way that was recognized by other countries until 1981 and Namibia in 1990.

In the postwar period there was a sustained period of European withdrawal from their colonies starting with the independence of India in 1947 and then

9 The term 'native' is now politically incorrect but I regard it as more accurate than the alternative 'indigenous.' Through its root the word does not commit to the idea of permanence as does 'indigeneity': an idea that is almost certainly unjustified for any identifiable 'people'.

10 In Angola, in 1972, three years before independence about 5% of the population was white. In Mozambique, it was 2%.

11 Namibia was the former German South West Africa, mandated to South Africa in the peace agreements after the First World War. But with the collapse of the League of Nations, South Africa had de facto absorbed it. After the Second World War the United Nations would repeatedly call on South Africa to give the colony its independence.

extending to most of Africa, the Middle East, the Caribbean, and South and Southeast Asia. As countries gained independence, calls to complete the process, particularly through motions of censure debated in the United Nations, became stronger. What emerged was a comradeship of recently independent countries willing to assist, sometimes materially and almost always through moral support. Closer to hand in Southern Africa, this would have real consequences for the South African economy as the flow of migrant labor from outside the country was disrupted. Malawi banned miner recruitment. There were also anxieties subsequent to Mozambican independence which pushed the Chamber of Mines recruiting apparatus to shift its emphasis towards South Africa itself.

As noted earlier, the South African case was different in other more fundamental and less conjunctural respects. In the first place, there was, on the part of the apartheid governments, both a desire to resist decolonization and an ability to resist. As far as desire was concerned, its colonial character had been, and was still believed by many, to be essential to maintaining its position in the international division of labor. A large white working class had been bought off into supporting the oppressions on which, it was believed, the profitability of the gold mines, and therefore South Africa's position in the global division of labor depended. It was a white working class that was, in a sense trapped since it enjoyed a high standard of living that was seen by many as dependent on the country's colonial structure.[12] There was also a power to resist. South Africa was colonial without being a colony in the formal sense. Rather it had been independent since 1910. Elsewhere where there had been a substantial white minority, as in Algeria or Kenya, the interests of the settlers had had to confront those of an imperial government which typically did not share their agenda with the same intensity. The settlers in South Africa did not have to stage a putsch, as they had to, with differing outcomes, in Algeria and Southern Rhodesia. Furthermore, the resources the South African government could call on in defending apartheid and resisting decolonization were not insubstantial. The white minority at about 15% of the total population in 1983, was relatively large and the country's economy had the heavy industry and technical knowledge that could be converted into military hardware of some sophistication.

Second, South Africa was of unusual strategic importance to the capitalist world. The country had become the major world supplier of the strategic

12 "A sobering fact which every opponent of apartheid should remember is that South African capital has proportionately a much larger popular base than virtually any other ruling class in the world. The five million middle and working class whites' huge material privileges are inseparable from white supremacy" (Callinicos, 1988a, p. 52).

minerals of chrome and platinum. Since the closure of the Suez Canal in 1967 and the development of major supertankers which were too large for the canal, it had also occupied a highly strategic position on one of the principal international oil routes in the world; something further dramatized by the presence of a major naval port at Simonstown close to Cape Town. There was also South Africa's crucial role as policeman in Southern Africa. This would become increasingly important in the 1980s as its own concerns about the so-called 'frontline states' came to mesh with those of the Reagan government's aggressive attempts to subvert anything deemed unfavorable to capitalism, whether it was in El Salvador, Nicaragua, Grenada, Afghanistan or, in Southern Africa, Angola or Mozambique. In Southern Africa, South Africa was the US's Cold War proxy fighting a war in Angola and supporting rebel movements in both Angola and Mozambique with a view to overturning governments seen, rightly or wrongly as favorable to Moscow.[13] For South Africa it was a matter of discouraging governments from supporting anti-apartheid forces which looked to them for the provision of material help and bases within striking distance of South Africa. For the US it was part of the grandiose mission of leading the so-called 'free world' in the defense of capitalism on a world scale (Gleijeses, 2014; 2016).

The third unusual feature of the South African case was its significance as a trading partner for Western firms. It was, after all, a middle-income country, huge income inequalities notwithstanding, and as such, an attractive market for consumer goods firms and for direct investment: among other things, American automobile companies had factories in South Africa. There was a stake in keeping South Africa in the capitalist camp and preempting social upheaval.[14]

This is not to imply that South Africa had been entirely obdurate. There was a sense in which the South African government bowed to the decolonizing wave, though it was no more than a reorganization of its institutional fix so as to enhance the state's legitimacy; a redefinition of where the country's boundary should be drawn. This was the homeland project which gathered momentum from the 1960s on and which was discussed in the last chapter. Africans would indeed be granted the vote, but not in South Africa itself. Rather they would be given their own nation states or 'homelands.' These would be carved out of the old native reserves dating back to the 1913 and 1936 Land Acts. They would enjoy citizenship there and they would enjoy the franchise, but not in

13 On the Mozambique case, see Hanlon (2010).

14 According to Harris (1986) this is one of the reasons that South Africa was able to negotiate relatively favorable refinancing terms in the wake of the 1985 crisis.

South Africa. Economic independence to match this political independence was something entirely different since the homelands would have to remain dependent on the remittances of migrant workers working within the newly drawn boundaries of a rump South Africa. There was an important sense in which the 'country' contracted geographically, therefore, without any serious challenge to the material relations on which its existence as a 'country' depended; but this was little different in a qualitative sense from the relation between France and its former West African colonies or that between the US and most of the Latin American countries, particularly those of Central America.

All this was thoroughly intended. Much less so were its implications for the development of resistance to the apartheid regime and intensified calls for a non-racial franchise. This was not because of any uprising in the homelands. Far from it, since for the most part their governments were bastions of conservatism and happy to join the apartheid government in its oppression of the African masses. Rather the problem lay with the unforeseen consequences of carrying out the homeland project to its logical end. This is because it entailed what was known as 'resettlement.' This in turn would result in a proletarianization of Africans and a rapid growth of the African labor movement which, along with urban youth and the civics would be one more thorn in the side of apartheid governments.

From the standpoint of the National Party, the move to create independent homelands was to resolve the issue of the African franchise once and for all. It was resolute that Africans should not enjoy the vote in South Africa itself. The homeland project was its way of bowing not just to external but also internal pressure: the demand of the ANC that all South Africans should have the right to vote for a unitary government regardless of race. In this sense the decolonization going on in the rest of the world was seen as an opportunity for the South African government. It too would decolonize, but on its own terms. If, however, it was to accomplish its purpose, then the Africans of South Africa had to become citizens of respective homelands. Simply formally announcing the fact of homelands that would eventually be independent would not do the trick if the geographic distribution of Africans remained what it was and if they could choose not to relocate into the homelands, which given their extreme poverty and dubious developmental outlook, was all the more likely. The answer would have to be a massive process of what has come to be known as 'ethnic cleansing' but which for the apartheid authorities went under the more benign term 'resettlement': a program of social engineering with quite appalling fallout in terms of human misery and impoverishment.

Africans in the 'white' rural areas bore the brunt of this.[15] This was the so-called 'whitening of the platteland' (Platzky and Walker, 1985). This meant in the first place that the reliance of the white farmer on Africans, as labor tenants or sharecroppers, had to be terminated once and for all. This was accomplished through a subsidized program of farm mechanization. Subsequently most of the now former sharecroppers, labor tenants, farm servants, could be literally defined as 'surplus people' – 'surplus' to the needs of white capital, that is – and be forcibly removed to the reserves-soon-to-be-homelands where they would join their so-called 'ethnic brothers and sisters.' Swelling this tide of human misery were the uprooted residents of the African peasant colonies that had been scattered across the 'white' rural areas: what were defined by the apartheid authorities, one assumes without irony, as 'black spots'.

But in the homelands there was no land for them and no work. Rather for most,[16] the only possibility of a livelihood was migrant labor: this required living in a hostel or with relatives in a 'white' city while dependents stayed behind. They were to form the core of a new type of migrant worker: one who had no alternatives and who came to be known as a 'career' migrant worker (Crush, 1989, pp. 19–20; 1995, p. 25). It is no coincidence that this was accompanied by a massive increase in union membership during the 1970s, and ultimately state recognition of African unions as negotiating agents; something that had been denied to them hitherto. This was especially the case in those sectors of the economy that had been dominated by migrant labor, notably the gold mining industry, but also the less skilled segments of manufacturing and in the docks.[17]

The organization of the African, the development of the labor movement, also spilled out beyond the metropolitan areas into towns located close by the homelands. As discussed in the last chapter, in its effort to staunch the movement of Africans to the major cities the government had introduced measures in the mid- to late-1960s to decentralize industrial employment to so-called 'growth points' in close proximity to the homelands. This was seen as a further step in the direction of 'whitening' South Africa, since Africans

15 The Section Tenners in urban areas were less vulnerable since they enjoyed legal rights of urban residence.

16 I have inserted the qualifier 'for most' since some would have found work through commuting to a nearby city. This was to become more important over time as homeland dwellers sought locations close to white cities so as to avoid migrant labor and separation from family.

17 In mining, as Crush (1989, pp. 19–20) points out, the professional migrant worker was encouraged since return to the same employer allowed imparting skills, exploiting experience, with the result of increased productivity.

would now become 'frontier commuters', as indeed they already were to some degree around Durban, East London, Newcastle, Pretoria and Bloemfontein. They lived in the homelands and worked in what the government hoped would eventually be a re-defined South Africa, stripped of its black appendages in the form of the, soon-to-be-independent, homelands. What was not anticipated, though, was that many of the relocated factories, typically branch plant operations, would become the focus of union organizing drives on the part of their African employees, as indeed occurred in growth points like Hammarsdale close to the KwaZulu border, and Rosslyn and Brits just south of Bophuthatswana boundaries.[18]

From the standpoint of the Western powers this was of limited moment. Rather they were willing to tolerate a racist regime regardless of popular pressures.[19] So long as it could provide a stable investment environment and continue to be a bastion of strength against communist takeovers in the area, the anti-apartheid movement would get only a limited hearing. That it did get a hearing is evident from the various boycott and divestment movements which were of real concern for apartheid governments in the 1980s. But the West was not willing to pull out the rug entirely from underneath South African governments until the crucial events of 1989–90 and the collapse of socialism-as-we-knew-it. This had several upshots, altering the balance of power in the struggle around decolonization in complex ways.

Not least, the West no longer needed a policeman in Southern Africa. Further, the ideological pretensions of anti-colonial movements and of the former colonial countries in Southern Africa, like those of Angola and Mozambique, were now called into question by the apparent triumph of the market. The anti-colonial forces could now be tamed and completing the neoliberal revolution in South Africa appeared more feasible. Better yet it could be a launching pad for a new regional initiative: that of extending the neoliberal revolution more widely. With the demise of apartheid African countries had no further reason for trade and investment boycotts of South African firms. The latter could now be the spearhead for demonstrating the virtues of the market.

18 See Stengel's (1990) account of how events unfolded in the Transvaal town of Brits and the consequences for the unionization of Africans.

19 It was ever thus. Compare Alex Callinicos (1988a) in his discussion of the aftermath of the crushing of the resistance to apartheid during the late 1950s and the banning of the ANC in 1960, following the banning of the South African Communist Party in 1950: "Once it became clear that the regime had been successful in crushing all black opposition, foreign capital poured into the country, attracted by the low wages and high profits, fueling a prodigious boom" (p. 16).

5 Interregnum

> The nationalization of the mines, banks and monopoly industries is the policy of the ANC, and the change or modification of our views in this regard is inconceivable. Black economic empowerment is a goal we fully support and encourage, but in our situation state control of certain sectors of the economy is unavoidable.
>
> MANDELA 'ANC Leader Affirms Support for State Control of Industry,' *Times* (London), January 26, 1990

> I do not intend to negotiate myself out of power
>
> FREDERIK DE KLERK

> Before transferring power, the Nationalist Party wants to emasculate it. It is trying to negotiate a kind of swap where it will give up the right to run the country its way in exchange for the right to stop blacks from running it their own way.
>
> ALLISTER SPARKS, South African journalist (in MURRAY, 1994, p. 1).

Going into the negotiations around a new constitution and, in effect, a new social settlement, for there were other concurrent negotiations around economic policy, which is significant in itself, the opposing forces were the African National Congress and the National Party. The ANC represented the African liberation movement and, on the other hand, the National Party, while recognizing that some concessions would have to be made, represented the forces of the status quo. The goal of the ANC was, at least in retrospect, to achieve a settlement in which Africans would control the state. State power, as per Mandela's quote above was seen as the key to implementing this program. It was a radical one that went back to the Freedom Charter of 1955 and reiterated by Mandela when he was released from prison. It was a program for the African masses, designed to control the wealth of the country with their interests in mind, calling for a sweeping program of nationalization of mining, industry and banks and a re-division of the land, putting aside the racial restrictions on ownership characteristic of the apartheid period.

The objective of the National Party, of course, was to resist this agenda, to limit ANC control of the state and what it could do with it, with the ultimate goal of protecting white privilege. This was not something, though, that would be settled purely in terms of the interests, admittedly class interests of

South Africans themselves. The stakes were far too high for that. Furthermore, the National Party would prove itself adept at harnessing more global forces, particularly of a discursive nature, to its cause. In this respect, and as a result of the concurrent demise of socialism as we knew it, the ANC would be seriously disadvantaged. The ideas of the right were in the ascendant and the left was disarmed. What would ensue would be indeed ANC control of the state, but a state that had been significantly transformed in its structural imperatives and which would not just compromise fulfillment of the Freedom Charter but would define them as utterly irrelevant to the future of the country: and despite Mandela's claim that 'modification of our views in this regard is inconceivable.'

For the World Bank, the IMF and for financial institutions more generally, interest in the outcome of the negotiations was intense. For the World Bank and the IMF this was partly the desire for a success story in Africa; an opportunity to show that an African state could indeed prosper, though on their terms. For financial institutions, particularly the international banks, a major concern was getting their money back from a state that, as a result of borrowings by apartheid governments, was highly indebted to them. What they all shared though was a desire to keep South Africa firmly in the capitalist camp, open to foreign investment and to money-making with minimum state interference, as they would have put it.[20]

In this respect of course they reflected the increasingly neo-liberal climate of the times both in terms of practice and discourse, and orchestrated by the major corporations, governments and technocrats of the developed world. This had been developing from at least the early 1980s as we saw above and had new wind in its sails as a result of the collapse of communist regimes in the Soviet Union and Eastern Europe and the clear turn to the market in China. The space was created for a new breed of technocrat, the so-called transitologists, who, either employed by global financial institutions or egged on by them, would do their work in not so much shoring up the economic status quo in South Africa as transforming it: eliminating regulations, like exchange controls, making state owned corporations available for foreign takeover and the like.

This required an ideological onslaught. An army of lawyers, economists sent by the WB and the IMF was put to work in seducing the ANC leadership. ANC staffers were drilled in 'economics' and recruited for periods of training in business schools in North America and Western Europe. They worked as interns

20 For a good summary of the sad history of decolonization see Khalili (2023).

in economic think tanks and in the WB itself.[21] The same was true with more specific programs like land reform, imparting a conventional wisdom through bringing the 'experts' down to South Africa and so justifying the protection of private property rights through appeals to arguments of a blandly technical character.

There was also a quite different set of arguments, fashioned again from theories of a supposedly universal nature, and once more providing leverage for a white settlerdom that on the ground was utterly outnumbered. Once again the goal was to frustrate a non-racial democracy. This was the idea of 'deeply divided societies' and the special political challenges posed by them. These were societies that were fractured along a variety of lines. These might include language (Belgium, Canada), religion (Netherlands, Northern Ireland) or both as in the case of Switzerland, Israel and the erstwhile Yugoslavia, and of course, race, including therefore South Africa and some might add the US. In contrast to the neo-liberal technocrats where economists and the occasional lawyer led the way, this was largely the preserve of political scientists, but as with the former, presenting themselves as disinterested observers: another view supposedly from nowhere. Aside from that, the concept is one of dubious coherence, but that has not impeded its mobilization in political combat.

This is because of its implications for constitution formation and this, of course, was at the heart of the negotiations in South Africa. Given intense social divisions, the view was that parliamentary democracy Westminster-style would have very serious limits. The sort of cross-cutting affiliations found in the most successful democracies and giving them a political stability that could co-exist with democracy were, it was argued, absent. What was needed was some sort of power sharing in which the scope for applying zero-sum solutions would be limited and all the different groups constituting the 'deeply divided society' would feel that their special needs and demands had been respected. The particular concept associated with this is Arend Lijphart's consociational democracy (1968) and, to be sure, Lijphart was keen to bring his ideas to the ongoing debate in South Africa.[22]

According to Lijphart (ibid) consociational democracy depended on the implementation of four particular constitutional features:

---

21 Comparison with the 're-education' programs of Maoist China is not that far-fetched.

22 "Since its initial formulation in the late-1960s consociationalism has led to a highly influential school of studies and consociational engineering has been marketed, particularly by Lijphart, as a genuinely attractive option to address the seemingly intractable ethnic divisions of South Africa" (Taylor, 1992, p. 1). 'Marketed' does not seem too strong a word.

a) Coalition government in which each of the different groups would participate.
b) The right of group veto or what was called 'concurrent majority rule.'
c) Proportional representation. The concern was that a minority with a fairly even geographic distribution – think South African whites – would not be represented under a first-past-the-post system.
d) A high degree of autonomy in 'own internal affairs.'

The latter, of course, recalls the attempt to 'reform' apartheid through the Constitutional Act of 1983. According to this, whites, Indians and Coloreds would each have autonomy in their 'own affairs': mainly health, housing and education. Africans were excluded since their future was supposed to lie in the homelands.[23] But Lijphart's arguments, arriving with the authority of international – more accurately, Western – political science, provided a respectability for the early negotiating position of the National Party that would otherwise have proven elusive.[24] There were pressures for group vetoes on legislation. To some degree, the view that consociationalism might be appropriate to the South African case deepened in the course of the negotiations. This was owing to an outbreak of what was referred to as 'black-on-black violence' though the idea that it might have been provoked by government agents – the so-called 'Third Force' – received a good deal of publicity at the time. Much of the violence was between Section Tenners and migrant workers in the hostels. Tensions between them had long been apparent in South Africa but now they were given an ethnic interpretation: many of the Section Tenners, particularly on the Rand where the violence was most intense, were of Xhosa origin while among the migrant workers Zulus tended to be overrepresented. The Inkatha (Zulu nationalist) party was deeply suspicious of the ANC, which it dubbed a Xhosa organization, and almost certainly played a part, perhaps with government help, in provoking the disturbances.[25]

This then played into the claims of a right-wing organization, the so-called Freedom Alliance: a coalition of right-wing Afrikaners and some homeland

23 Though a bone had been thrown to the Section Tenners in the form of the black municipality act which gave them an elective form of government replacing the Administration Boards of the central government.

24 There is a more general point here: The advice of academics is sought because of the air of objectivity concealing the *status quo* nature of their theories.

25 The Durban area was different: hostel dwellers and the permanently urbanized were both Zulu. In addition, among the migrant workers, geography played an important role in the degree to which they identified with the Inkatha Freedom Party (Cox and Hemson, 2008).

leaders who, realizing that the homelands would be abolished under the new constitution favored by the ANC, sought to oppose it. Their demand was for a confederal constitution that, building on the homelands, would include a white homeland, thus satisfying one of the criteria for a consociational democracy. It was not taken seriously but it did make the debate about the new constitution more complex and underlined the intensity of some of the cleavages, something which the National Party took advantage of.

The discourse of neo-liberalism, though, would turn out to be far more important, helping to impose a settlement to the advantage of private property and international corporate interests as opposed to those of the South African working class which, of course, comprised dominantly people of color. Notable features would include:[26]

- A liberalized trading regime: South Africa would join the General Agreement on Tariffs and Trade (GATT) and its successor the World Trade Organization (WTO). This would mandate elimination of the subsidies hitherto provided to its textiles and automobile industries. In combination with the lowering of tariff barriers, this would generate considerable unemployment, notably in the former.
- An independent central bank: The idea here was to put it at a distance from democratic controls when this was still a pipedream among the free market ideologues. The justification was to remove the bank from 'politics' or rather a particular sort of politics that might challenge capital's pretensions to an uncompromising domination.
- Elimination of currency controls: This was the result of an IMF agreement signed before the elections of 1994 in exchange for a $850M loan. The agreement was for a phased reduction over a number of years. It would result in massive disinvestment from South Africa.
- A private property clause in the constitution: In the event this would turn out to be – in fact was thoroughly intended as – a serious obstacle to land reform in that it eliminated the possibility of expropriation without compensation.
- An agreement to pay back the debt incurred by apartheid governments: This was completed even while the international banks that had made the loans could legitimately be argued to have, in so doing, prolonged the agony of the South African masses. This then lent force to the privatization of state-owned industries (Klein, 2007, p. 212), most notably iron and steel and oil-from-coal (SASOL) since their sale

26 For a stunning critique of this see Naomi Klein (2007, Chapter 10).

> generated money that could pay down the debt.[27] It also meant a loan from the IMF, as per the reference above, with all that that would entail for increasing the vulnerability of the South African economy to external pressures.

These measures would then set the scene for the incorporation of South Africa into a particular understanding of economic development. At the heart of this would be ideas about the importance of inward investment, trickle-down and therefore of maintaining an attractive 'business climate.' Economic development would become a technical matter beyond the reach of partisan debate, or so it was hoped. And South Africa would be the latest addition to the global league tables enshrined in the idea of benchmarking.

One can only speculate why an ANC that was still committed to the Freedom Charter at the beginning of the negotiations allowed itself to be put in this position and to have its policy options for future African-majority rule so utterly compromised. With the end of the Cold War the discursive environment might have lent the Freedom Charter a somewhat archaic feel. Race might also have factored into the vulnerability of the ANC to the arguments of the experts; not least the feeling that, in the context of failures elsewhere on the continent, Africans had something to prove; that they had to be exemplary pupils. But then ANC membership extended beyond Africans. The cave-in of white communists like Joe Slovo adds to the perplexity. As for Mandela, one hesitates to attribute too much significance to his volte-face. He has certainly been the subject of some recent reassessment and not always very flattering. How committed he ever was to a radical agenda has been questioned (Freund, 2014, p. 293). He has been constructed as a moderating influence (Beresford, 2014) who steered South Africa away from the precipice of civil war, but certainly not as a person who radically reordered the country's power structure (McKinley, 2023; Richburg, 2024).

The arguments about South Africa as a so-called 'deeply divided society' and what to do about it would be less apparent in the settlement but nevertheless of some importance. Aside from a grand coalition government which would be purely transitional, their most notable expression was the adoption of proportional representation. This allowed an ongoing voice for class privilege and a mitigation of the anxieties of international capital. Henceforth, privileged whites would secure more political representation than first-past-the-post

27 So, as Naomi Klein (2007) points out, instead of the nationalization promised by the Freedom Charter, the ANC presided over a de-nationalization.

would have allowed. If they had been more geographically concentrated it would have mattered less.

In conclusion, what deserves emphasis in understanding the outcome of the negotiations is the role of more global, discursive pressures, in alliance with representatives of the old regime, keen to take advantage of internal disorders of a seemingly territorial sort, so as to make South Africa safe for capital. But both sets of pressures that I have identified here – those of the neo-liberal variety and the claims about 'deeply divided societies' and what to do about them, can be seen to de-contextualize. South Africa was and continues to be put into slots which marginalize its particularly brutal character, abstracting from the particularities of the place and the distinctive nature of its class politics. Meanwhile international social science with its aura of objectivity was able to do its work. As Ben Fine (2008) observed in introducing a lecture on the peculiarities of the South African economy: "I have always been wary of telling South Africans about their own economy as my harshest criticism of other economists is for those – from the World Bank through to the latest Harvard group advising, or legitimizing, Treasury – who impose preconceived and generally flawed ideas on the South African economy rather than starting from its economic realities".

And likewise from Connors (1996) in a discussion of consociational democracy and its applicability to South Africa:

> it is wishful and Utopian to think of a 'true' consociationalism. Models are rarely grafted on to complex realities in toto. Models are better understood as reifications of social processes emptied of their historical and dynamic features. Lijphart wished to make patterns of consociationalism in Europe generalizable, without showing much appreciation of the historical and ideological processes that led to their emergence.
>
> (p. 23); see TAYLOR (1992) for a similar conclusion

A country which others tried to make in their own preferred images, therefore: images which would certainly not work to the advantage of the South African masses, as we will see in the chapter to follow.

CHAPTER 5

Decolonizing South Africa: A Hiding to Nothing

1 Introduction

In the (geo)history of South Africa, 1994 is not such a caesura as is often depicted. During the 1980s, there had already been change of a decolonizing nature, if hesitant and within limits. This included the rescinding of influx control and job reservation. There was also an ongoing transformation of the racial franchise, as in the 1983 Constitution Act and the black municipalities. The election of, first, a coalition government with the National Party and then the majority rule of the ANC, would give accelerated impetus to this process. However: We should note just how difficult decolonization is, particularly in settler societies like South Africa, with a prolonged history of white domination and the subordination, material and political, of the non-'European' masses. Materially, it is a matter of overturning colonial structures of domination, not just formal equality but real equality of a decolonizing sort in state and economy; a state and economy indifferent to color. This has to go with a decolonizing of the mind: weaning the masses away from the idea that the white person knows best; as, remarkably, in the way the negotiations over a new constitution proceeded – not least, far too much credence given to the self-serving blandishments of white institutions like the IMF and the multiple American 'consultants.' But also, and paradoxically, undoing the idea of white people – at least those of South Africa – as an unmitigated negative force, as in the desire of the ANC to overturn Bantu education which, as will be suggested, was entirely misplaced; and then the 'African' solutions for treating HIV-AIDS.

There are glaring issues of equity in reconstructing South Africa, but it remains only a middle-income country, which means that there are limits to what can be accomplished without economic growth; something accentuated by the inevitable opposition of the privileged, largely white, minority, to any redistribution of a radical nature. The trajectory can be described as, initially, one of progress. This has been followed by serious stagnation, even retrogression, with the vandalization of the country's physical infrastructure and the descent into corruption of public office. Geohistory has once again mattered, not only in an objective situation beyond the control of the government that has made growth difficult: not least the rise of China and a location in the southern hemisphere that works to the disadvantage of other countries, including the Southern Cone and even Australasia; but also in the way corruption has taken

 | DOI:10.1163/9789004715585_006

over, while easy explanations in terms of how it is just 'Africa', should rightly be rejected.

Corruption is a huge problem and one that clearly impacts on economic growth; not least by discouraging investment. In this penultimate chapter, I abstract from it to focus first on questions of distribution, both in the usual sense of the material, and in the less common one of securing recognition for all (Fraser, 2000): just what has been accomplished so far in the improvement of housing, education, better jobs, for the masses. This is followed by a discussion of the postcolonial state in South Africa, emphasizing not just its democratic shortfall – less democratic than it might seem, even while the racial franchise has been abolished; but also the failure to secure mass consent through a unifying national project. The latter is then prefatory to a discussion of why, even without a corrupt state, a dynamic growth course would have been challenging. The question of corruption, on the other hand, raises that of state failure; something to be addressed in the final chapter.

2 An Audit of the New South Africa

2.1 *Race and Material Conditions*

The first thing we should note is the way in which race continues to structure economic life. Over four-fifths of all commercial farmland is still owned by whites. There is a land reform program. Its intention was to transfer 30% of all white-owned land into black hands by 2014, but by 2018 barely one-third of that had been redistributed. The same applies to the employee-employer relation. For the vast majority of Africans, Coloreds and Indians in the private sector, the employer is still likely to be white. And of course, among the employees, race continues as a major predictor of what a person does and what she earns.

In the period since 1994 the distribution of different occupations across the four population groups has barely budged. Table 7 provides comparative data over the ten-year period between 1996 and 2006 on the proportions of the different population groups in the four highest-earning occupational categories:

Table 8 brings the story up to date but with a different set of occupational categories since the earlier ones were unavailable. The message, though, is very similar. Several things stand out. Obviously, whites are still hugely advantaged and Africans disadvantaged and with some hint that, for the latter, things may have slightly deteriorated. The other thing is how the population groups divide into two: the occupational profile of Indians is much closer to that of whites, while that for the Coloreds, more like that of the Africans.

TABLE 7 Occupations amongst the employed aged 15–65 years by population group: figures are percentages within each population group

	Africans		Coloreds		Indians		Whites	
	1996	2006	1996	2006	1996	2006	1996	2006
Legislators, senior officials and managers	1.7	2.3	2.7	2.3	7.5	14.5	11.1	19.4
Professionals	7.5	2.8	6.6	1.3	11.5	8.4	17.1	10.8
Technicians and associate Professionals	3.1	7.3	4.9	7.2	10.0	12.7	14.4	14.5
Clerks	4.4	6.2	9.3	9.7	14.8	18.4	15.9	20.0

SOURCE: STATSSA HOUSEHOLD SURVEYS 1996 AND 2006

TABLE 8 Occupational composition by population group, 2009, 2015, 2019

	Africans			Coloreds			Indians			Whites		
	2009	2015	2019	2009	2015	2019	2009	2015	2019	2009	2015	2019
Skilled	16.2	15.5	16.8	22.0	18.0	20.0	44.9	48.3	48.0	60.5	59.5	62.0
Semi-skilled	48.0	49.1	49.4	50.5	49.0	48.4	50.1	46.3	46.8	37.2	37.5	35.7
Low-skilled	35.9	35.4	33.8	27.4	33.0	31.6	5.1	5.4	5.2	2.3	3.0	2.3

SOURCES: FOR 2009 AND 2015: HTTPS://WWW.STATSSA.GOV.ZA/PUBLICATIONS/REPORT-02-11-02/REPORT-02-11-022015.PDF. (ACCESSED JULY 7, 2024). FOR 2019: HTTP://WWW.STATSSA.GOV.ZA/PUBLICATIONS/REPORT-02-11-02/REPORT-02-11-022019.PDF. (ACCESSED JULY 7, 2024)

These occupational differences are also reflected in data on income distribution (Table 9). This indicates the distribution of all salary-earners classified by population group across the five quintiles of the total income distribution

TABLE 9 Percent of population groups in each quintile of the total income distribution in South Africa 2015

Quintile	Africans	Coloreds	Indians	Whites
1	12.4	20.9	43.9	74.9
2	19.4	25.3	33.1	18.2
3	21.5	26.9	14.6	4.5
4	23.0	17.2	6.4	1.3
5	23.8	9.6	2.0	1.1

SOURCE: STATISTICS SOUTH AFRICA (2015, P. 21) LIVING CONDITIONS OF HOUSEHOLDS IN SOUTH AFRICA. PRETORIA. AVAILABLE HERE: HTTPS://WWW.STATSSA.GOV.ZA/PUBLICATIONS/P0310/P03102014.PDF. (ACCESSED JULY 7, 2024)

for 2015.[1] What is very clear from this is the way in which the racial hierarchy continues to be an income hierarchy. The domination of the first quintile by whites jumps out. Africans tend to be distributed fairly evenly across all quintiles with a mild tendency for their representation to increase with increasing quintile. The Indian distribution, on the other hand, is much more similar to the white one.

What this neglects, of course are the large numbers of South Africans in the working years who are not actually working. The rate of unemployment is quite staggering. Depending on how one calculates the unemployment rate, it can vary between 27% and 40%. This means that many, and they are mostly African, have to survive on very little income at all. According to World Bank figures for 2020, well over half the population was living in what the South African state defined as poverty, and a quarter experienced food poverty.[2]

This is not to say that material circumstances have not been equalized to some degree. The replacement of whites in the civil service, both national, provincial and local has been hugely formative of an African middle class, not to

1 The data are not as up-to-date as I would prefer but material in a similar format for more recent years proved elusive.

2 https://databankfiles.worldbank.org/public/ddpext_download/poverty/33EF03BB-9722-4AE2-ABC7-AA2972D68AFE/Global_POVEQ_ZAF.pdf (Accessed July 7, 2024).

TABLE 10 Percentages living in formal housing[a]

Africans			Coloreds			Indians			Whites		
1996	2006	2015	1996	2006	2015	1996	2006	2015	1996	2006	2015
49.4	60.8	65.3	90.4	88.7	N.A.	91.9	95.7	N.A.	96.2	94.1	N.A.

a Individual brick structures; flats in a block of flats; or a town/cluster or semi-detached house
SOURCE: STATSSA HOUSEHOLD SURVEYS; CALCULATED BY AUTHOR

mention Colored and Indian. Wages and salaries are significantly higher than in the private sector: R11,668 for the average public sector worker vs R7,822 for the private sector equivalent, or almost fifty percent higher. A much higher rate of unionization (70% of formal public sector workers vs 36% in the private sector) has then maintained the difference, as well as increasing the wage at a regular pace.[3]

Another notable advance, and one that has been less noticed, has been the de-racialization of pensions. There were old age pensions under apartheid but they were, like everything else, racially scaled. White pensions were considerably in excess of those granted to Colored and Indian people and Africans fared least well of all (see Table 1 in Chapter 1.) On the other hand, the process of de-racializing pensions started in the closing years of apartheid. Pensions have now been equalized across the different population groups, and upwards. This has been hugely important for many African households where, often, the granny is the only person receiving any income at all. It has likewise given some impulse, albeit mild, to the growth of entrepreneurial activity in the most rural and poorest parts of Africa where traders in the informal sector set up their stalls around the distribution center on pension day.

Despite the fact that large numbers of Africans still live in shacks and other sorts of 'informal' housing, conditions overall have undoubtedly improved (Table 10). A hallmark of post-apartheid governments has been a concerted attempt to provide formal housing structures. This has worked through once-in-a-lifetime grants to households towards the purchase of a lot and structure. The grants have been quite modest and so are the houses that are typically built on them, and, to minimize land costs, typically distant from where the jobs are, but they are structurally sound and can be added to as family circumstances improve.

3 Siphiwe Sibeko, 'South Africa's civil servants are the country's new labor elite.' The Conversation, February 18, 2016. Available here: https://theconversation.com/south-africas-civil-servants-are-the-countrys-new-labour-elite-54269 (Accessed July 7, 2024).

TABLE 11 Percentage of all households with electricity for cooking

Africans			Coloreds			Indians			Whites		
1996	2006	2015	1996	2006	2015	1996	2006	2015	1996	2006	2015
31.5	50.2	78.5	72.6	83.1	90.4	98.0	96.7	92.7	100.0	96.1	87.8

SOURCE: STATSSA HOUSEHOLD SURVEYS; CALCULATED BY AUTHOR. WHITE AND INDIAN DECLINES ALMOST CERTAINLY DUE TO TAKE UP OF GAS

TABLE 12 Percentage of all households with electric lighting

Africans			Coloreds			Indians			Whites		
1996	2006	2015	1996	2006	2015	1996	2006	2015	1996	2006	2015
46.4	74.2	89.0	83.2	90.4	97.0	98.6	98.4	98.9	99.1	98.1	99.6

SOURCE: STATSSA HOUSEHOLD SURVEYS; CALCULATED BY AUTHOR

The housing program is one of the reasons for the progress made in extending electricity to African households and to a lesser degree Coloreds (Tables 11 and 12), and then the extension of mains water (Table 13).

Nevertheless, urban land for those Africans lacking formal housing remains a big and growing problem. The challenge is finding land on which to erect a shack, in a context where invasion of public land is monitored and often dealt with through demolition. By 2018 there were indications that land invasions for purposes of housing – private and public land, both – had increased; certainly

TABLE 13 Percentage of all households, with piped water in house, yard or access to public tap, by percent of population group total

Africans			Coloreds			Indians			Whites		
1996	2006	2015	1996	2006	2015	1996	2006	2015	1996	2006	2015
74.4	77.6	84.3	96.4	95.9	97.9	97.5	97.4	98.4	98.5	95.3	96.1

SOURCE: STATSSA HOUSEHOLD SURVEYS; CALCULATED BY AUTHOR

they received a huge amount of publicity. The resistance to land occupations has not just been by the authorities. In some cases land that was reserved for permanent structures has been invaded to the great chagrin of those who stood to be rehoused from adjacent shacks. In other cases the opposition has come from upwardly mobile Africans anxious about their property values. In still others, existing shack dwellers next to the invaded land have risen up in opposition in virtue of the ways in which land invasions are often politicized and violent: so ANC or EFF (Economic Freedom Fighters) fighting for leadership of the invasion to secure votes.

Adding to the stress on urban land have been firstly the refugee crisis, particularly refugees from Zimbabwe; and the expulsion of Africans from white farms. It is a common view that the Extension of Security of Tenure Act of 1997, which extended labor legislation to agriculture, led to evictions and dismissals. Just how significant the act was in promoting an exodus of Africans from the white rural areas is hard to estimate, particularly given ambiguities in the statistics: some include domestic workers under calculations of agricultural employment and some do not. But while according to the Department of Agriculture, Forestry and Fisheries, in 1996 there were 914,500 agricultural workers in the country,[4] by 2010 there had been a dramatic decline of almost 44% to just over 500,000 workers.

2.2 *The Skills Problem*

The skills problem in South Africa is one of the most pressing that the country faces. It affects not just the private sector and its need for machinists, engineers, software specialists, lathe operators, and all manner of expertise and experience. It also affects the state. So-called 'state capacity' is a major challenge for the country and the state's skills base is part of what is being referred to. Decolonization requires a multi-faceted attack on much of the colonial structure, including local and provincial government. The risk of incompetence and behavior that is downright unprofessional is one of the reasons that the ANC has tried to maintain firm control from the center, though this has made it vulnerable to arguments that it is trying to take over the state and, anyway, it only works if the central state is not just as incompetent.

The fact is, of course, that for much of the existence of the South African state since 1910 the education of that vast African majority has been parlous. Prior to apartheid, the only schools available to Africans were the mission

4 https://www.daff.gov.za/daffweb3/portals/0/statistics%20and%20economic%20analysis/statistical%20information/abstract%202016%20.pdf (Accessed July 7, 2024).

schools. These were underfunded and their presence very far from universal. Part of the reason for this neglect was the racist view that the African was impervious to formal education. It was also the view that in South Africa's colonial framework, what was needed from the African was the lower forms of labor, and plenty of it.[5] And job reservation made aspiration beyond that futile.

It is true that from the late 1970s on, state expenditure on African education did indeed increase quite remarkably, and this has continued into post-apartheid times. One result is that in terms of inputs, Africans are getting more education than they ever did. Table 14 tells part, but only part, of the story. It charts the highest levels of education people achieved for the different population groups and for four years, 1996, 2005, 2015 and 2018, though note that the age groups are not comparable between 1996–2005 and 2015–2018. The lowest education level corresponds to 'no schooling' at all, while the highest refers to people with some sort of university degree. Africans have clearly moved up the education ladder and to a lesser degree, so too have Coloreds. For Africans there has been a drop in the proportion failing to make it beyond Level 2 and a noticeable increase in those staying on to Level 3. On the other hand, much remains to be done. The racial hierarchy is still very evident, even for those in the younger age cohort. To be white still means to be 'more educated' on average, and by a very considerable margin. Again, Indians are closer to whites and the Colored statistics track more closely the numbers for Africans.

This assumes, of course, that simple attendance has meaning in terms of what the education economists would call 'outputs.' This is a huge assumption. Despite major advances in terms of equalizing the spending of money per pupil and in closing the racial gap in terms of the levels to which education is taken, results remain disappointing. Historically, variations in pupil-teacher ratios were very substantial indeed and followed the racial hierarchy, but evening these out does not seem to have had much effect on exam results. A crucial benchmark is the school leaving or 'matriculation' exam. On its outcome depends not only whether a student will be allowed to proceed to university or even whether or not he or she can enter anything other than the most menial of employment, if that.

5 As the complete quotation from Hendrik Verwoerd made clear, and putting his notorious remark about a seeming African deficiency in a somewhat different light: "There is no place for [the Bantu] in the European community above the level of certain forms of labour … What is the use of teaching the Bantu child mathematics when it cannot use it in practice? That is quite absurd. Education must train people in accordance with their opportunities in life, according to the sphere in which they live"; which puts a slightly different blush on a quote typically drawn on to underline a more visceral sort of racism.

TABLE 14 Highest education levels attained by population group 20–30 for 1996 and 2005; over 20 for 2015 and 2018

Education level	Africans				Coloreds				Indians				Whites			
	1996	2005	2015	2018	1996	2005	2015	2018	1996	2005	2015	2018	1996	2005	2015	2018
1	19.5	16.1	6.4	4.5	11.1	9.7	3.0	3.4	6.0	3.1	1.9	1.4	1.4	0.2	0.4	0.1
2	29.5	28.1	17.2	14.5	31.7	32.7	21.6	24.4	14.4	12.5	3.4	3.8	1.4	1.4	1.5	0.9
3	46.3	49.3	66.3	68.8	50.6	52.1	67.5	55.5	67.3	67.2	63.1	67.5	65.4	65.1	58.6	52.6
4	3.7	5.2	6.9	8.5	5.6	4.8	7.6	11.0	7.0	9.9	13.6	11.0	19.3	20.7	17.0	22.5
5	0.9	1.4	3.2	3.6	1.0	0.7	3.2	0.6	5.3	7.3	17.9	16.3	12.5	12.7	22.5	23.9

a For 1996 and 2005: Level 1: no schooling; Level 2: Grades 1, 2 and Standards 1–5; Level 3: Standards 6–10; Level 4: National Technical Certification I, II and III, diplomat/certification with Standard 9 or lower or with Standard 10 (1996); or: certificate with less than Grade 12 / Standard 10 Diploma with less than Grade 12 / Standard 10 Certificate with Grade 12 / Standard 10 Diploma with Grade 12 / Standard 10 (2005); Level 5: university degree

b For 2015: Level 1: no schooling; Level 2: Grades 1, 2 and Standards 1–5; Level 3: Standards 6–10; Level 4: National Technical Certification I, II and III; or: Certificate with less than Grade 12 / Standard 10; Certificate with Grade 12 / Standard 10; Diploma with less than Grade 12 / Standard 10; Diploma with Grade 12 / Standard 10; Level 5: university degree

c For 2019: Level 4: National Technical Certification I, II and III; or: Certificate with less than Grade 12; Occupation Certificate Level 5; Certificate with Grade 12; Diploma with Grade 10; Higher Diploma

SOURCES: STATSSA HOUSEHOLD SURVEYS; CALCULATED BY AUTHOR

The good news is that since the accession of a black-majority government in 1994, the number of African students actually taking the matriculation exam has increased by about fifty percent: testimony to the effort placed on improving access to formal education for all races. The bad news is that the same old racial differences persist. Pass rates are a function of race. Over one third of African students failed in 2003 compared with about 10% or less for the three other population groups. The white failure rate was negligible. That was some while ago. Since then, data have been difficult to obtain, which may be significant in itself, but a report from the 2016 South Africa Survey published by the Institute of Race Relations[6] suggests that the differences continue.

Part of the reason for these continuing distinctions has to do with resources. Despite the money put into African education, there are still disparities. These in turn are a result of a peculiarity of the South African educational system which deserves extended comment. First, it is important to note that all so-called public schools in South Africa are supported in part by fees paid by parents. These fees are set by a governing body made up of parents, and the school principal. This means that fees can be used by the wealthy to exclude the poor, and since most of the poor are Africans, to exclude Africans in particular. Schools in richer white areas have much higher fees than those in poorer white areas or in the townships. In an expensive, formerly all-white suburb, a high school may charge fees well beyond what most Africans, or Coloreds and Indians for that matter, can afford. Township schools, on the other hand, will typically have fees that are much, much lower.

Reinforcing this exclusionary tendency, schools have feeder or catchment areas, and must give priority to pupils living there. In a context of residential segregation by income and still considerably by race, this means that segregation will be reflected in the pupil compositions of different schools. This does not mean that children from other areas cannot attend a particularly good school: just that they can only be admitted if there is room. The transport costs for children from the townships to the 'better' schools will then add considerably to those that must already be met in the form of fees. Children are brought in, but their parents have to have the money to do it.

Higher fees not only exclude. They also translate into better, more qualified, more experienced teachers and into much better facilities as well. The 'better' schools simply have more money to spend on computers, sports facilities,

6 Commentary here: http://www.acts.co.za/news/blog/2016/02/racial-inequalities-show-up-in-matric-results. (Accessed July 7, 2024).

libraries. They cannot pay teachers more but they can pick and choose them, since only the most dedicated will forgo the opportunity to work with the better facilities available in the more privileged schools. Not only that, they can hire more teachers and so drive down the pupil-teacher ratio.[7]

Quite why this bizarre situation continues given the government's so-called 'transformational' goals is something to be taken up later in this chapter. For the time being we should note how the subsequent differences reinforce those that result from what the educational sociologists call, rather euphemistically, 'family background.' Family circumstances are important in giving children an early start and a cultural formation that can complement that acquired in the public school system. If both parents have full-time jobs that leave them exhausted when they get home, then there is little likelihood of creative time devoted to the children. Family income tends to affect the exposure of children to books and a reading culture, as well as what is watched on television. The more money there is, the more likely there will be family travel and the stimulus that that can bring.[8]

The result of this skills deficit is that the government constantly runs up against the limits of what it can do. It wants to transfer land to Africans and it wants to see the emergence of a black business class but it is stymied. Its plans are quickly exposed as built on little more than sand and it has to slow down. One of the reasons that land reform has lagged so much is that what is called 'aftercare' – which includes technical advice of an agronomic and business nature – just is not available. Land has been returned to former African owners but subsequent to their previous dispossession many have dropped out of farming and have very little idea as to what it entails. This is particularly the case given the vast changes in agricultural technology and the fact that they must now produce competitively for the market and not just for themselves.

---

7 One effect of these arrangements is that racial desegregation has assumed a very particular form. In Durban, the children in a formerly all-white school who are not white are likely to be Indian; their parents are better off, and given the residential geography bequeathed by the implementation of the Group Areas Act, they are more likely to be living close by or even in the same feeder area. It is in formerly Indian schools, on the other hand, that one is particularly likely to see African children (alongside Indians). This is largely because, while the quality of the education will be higher than that in the township schools, the fees will be lower, reflecting what the majority of Indians can afford (i.e., less than what the majority of whites can afford).

8 In discussing the skills deficit, reference should also be made to the HIV-AIDS crisis in the first decade of this century. Since 2010, greater access to retro-virals and shifts in behavior have brought down the rate of infection very considerably, but there are serious after-effects: most notably a massive population of orphans.

The result has been some major disasters and a mood of 'I told you so' among those white farmers who were hostile to the land reform program from the beginning.

The attempt to create a black business class has likewise stumbled and one has to think that this is because the government was in too much of a hurry to allow it to emerge more organically, learning as it went. It may be, of course, that the government was correct and that given the lack of skills among Africans and Coloreds in particular, engineering, professional, managerial, entrepreneurial, organic growth would have taken a very, very long time indeed, if ever. Meanwhile what has been created is a class of people who receive property income in virtue of some ownership stake in a business but do very little to earn it, except to have the right connections with the government and a black skin.

The procedure has been one in which white owned firms have been pressured to sell stock to what usually turn out to be well positioned Africans. The stock is paid for by a loan taken out by the African in question with the stock as collateral. The assumption has been that it would increase in value over time so that recipients would have no difficulty paying back the loan. In many cases it has not, and the banks have been placed in the awkward position of either looking the other way or repossessing the stock and so risking the political opprobrium of the government. Where firms have been established by what are called the 'historically disadvantaged', the government has allowed them to tender for state business for sums in excess of those offered by white-owned firms. This, however, has also backfired since it encourages the formation of what are essentially companies in name only which, once the contract has been secured, sub-contract to white firms. In short, policies have encouraged black ownership and the business viability of black owned firms, but, and this should be emphasized, not black entrepreneurship.[9]

9 According to a report to the Helen Suzman Foundation: "Black businessmen have been roundly criticized both by Mbeki and finance minister Trevor Manuel for "not adding value" and for acting as mere rentier capitalists, holding shares in white companies that do the actual work – or as token black faces in tender bids. Dikgang Moseneke has pointed out that many black businessmen concentrated on owning shares and becoming directors, usually implying a hands-off approach to the actual operational management of an enterprise. Yet it was precisely in the sphere of operational management that all real influence lay and all real skills were learned and developed. Bheki Sibiya, executive director of Transnet, says that 'black empowerment initiatives will never succeed unless African communities receive proper business training.'" Full report here: https://hsf.org.za/publications/focus/issue-17-first-quarter-2000/black-economic-empowerment. (Accessed July 7, 2024).

2.3 *Transitioning the State*

The crucial label for the South African state now is 'post-colonial.' This has numerous meanings and lots of baggage. The least troublesome is the literal one: that apartheid was a colonial state, not in the sense of representing Her Majesty's Government, or whatever, but as the tool of a settler minority, and that it has now been replaced by one that governs, hopefully, on behalf of all; all of which, of course, is symbolized by the shift from a racial franchise to a universal one.

South Africa is formally democratic. Yet while the suffrage is universal, the rules governing elections are more ambiguous in their effects. On the one hand, the fact of proportional representation means that everybody has a voice missing from the more common 'first-past-the-post' and the problem of wasted votes. On the other, while there are rules governing party finance, they are less encouraging. This is because they can be worked around, meaning that there are no limits to what a party can spend in an election campaign, so long as it can raise the money. Likewise, while the constitution provides for checks and balances, this is only formal, and the independence of the judiciary has become an issue.This leads us back to the post-colonial condition and in a sense that is enduring and that has been particularly important in South Africa. This is understanding politics in colonial terms: of a (one-time) oppressed majority versus a (one-time) settler minority that controlled their lives. There is, in other words, a temptation to conduct politics in a retaliatory sort of way: to replace white nationalism with an African version; to treat other non-indigenes like Indians and Coloreds as exactly that – a little more sympathetically than under apartheid, but nevertheless second-class citizens (Mamdani, 2001). And yet, one should be careful in how these matters are judged.

Nationalism is important since it is the cultural glue that gives a state legitimacy. It is something that is purposefully manipulated by the state, even while the state has to work within inherited limits. Initially in South Africa the ANC-dominated state trod very carefully. This was the honeymoon period of the rainbow nation with some nice stage-managed symbolic acts like Mandela wrapping himself in the jersey of the national rugby team: important because of its centrality to Afrikaner nationalism. There was good reason for treading carefully. It was clear that South Africa could only be reconstructed with the help of the existing technical and managerial cadres and these happened to be largely white. But in a context of strongly opposed visions of a future South Africa, concocting a national story acceptable to all was very difficult indeed. In the words of Adam, Slabbert and Moodley (1997, p. 103) "creating a South African nation has to do with walking a fine line between politically and constitutionally recognizing cultural pluralism and diversity and developing overarching symbols of solidarity and commitment transcending particular ethnic loyalties." The idea of the 'rainbow nation' was a fallback position.

There are real problems here. For the longest while, it seemed that neither white nor black faces could appear on banknotes in South Africa. In lieu of some willingness to accept each other's heroes as 'creators of modern South Africa' – Paul Kruger, Govan Mbeki, Ruth First, Cecil Rhodes, Mahatma Gandhi, Abdullah Abdurahman, Walter Luthuli, perhaps – resort has been to rather anodyne images of the country's wildlife. Subsequent to the passing of Mandela, this policy has now been breached, but it remains the exception. The same sensitivity applies to postage stamps. The difficulties of putting together a revised history curriculum for South African schools can only be imagined.

Common symbols are hard to find. What resonates with whites does not resonate with Africans, Indians or Coloreds and vice versa. Significantly, and allowing for the dated statistics of some twenty years ago, but testifying to the tentativeness with which the government has proceeded in this area, it was whites who were the most likely to identify as 'South African,' though Indians and Coloreds were not far behind (see Table 15). It was, rather, Africans who were least likely to identify as South Africans and to a quite remarkable degree: less than half, apparently. The obvious symbols shared by most South Africans have to do with their common history of suffering at the hands of the white settlers, but clearly, as with any serious policy of income redistribution, this is forbidden territory.

TABLE 15 How South Africans identify themselves

	Black	Colored	Indian or Asian	White	Total
% of Total	75%	8%	3%	14%	100%
'An African'	23%	4%	4%	5%	18%
'A South African'	44%	78%	70%	82%	53%
'Black / White / Colored / Indian'	3%	12%	18%	4%	4%
'Zulu / Xhosa / Swazi / English / Dutch'	18%	1%	0%	2%	14%

SOURCE: FUTUREFACT PEOPLESCAPE 2004 SURVEY

Even so, there have been attempts to assert a more exclusively African identity as what South Africa is about. 1999 and the election of Thabo Mbeki as President represents something of a watershed. Most notably he talked about an African Renaissance in which he hoped that South Africans would adopt an African identity, though there was always some ambiguity as to who the South Africans were: just Africans, or also Colored, Indians and whites? There were also some tentative steps towards Africanization at a symbolic level. So in some remarkable tits-for-tats, place names are being Africanized and those named after Afrikaner heroes or apartheid figures are renamed, sometimes after the worthies of the ANC. Pietersburg becomes Polokwane, Pretoria, Tshwane, Port Elizabeth, Mandela, and Durban eThekwini, while the former Jan Smuts International Airport in Johannesburg is now the Oliver Tambo International Airport. As Maré (2005, p. 509) has written: "Renaming towns, cities, streets, and removing as well as erecting statues and monuments to other, previously demonized political figures serve as mirror images to previous practices. The imagination to rethink diversity is lacking, and the old common sense with new content prevails."

In retrospect, Africanization under Mbeki was pretty harmless stuff. Under his successor Jacob Zuma things took a decidedly more toxic turn. This was not in the sense of alienating whites as it was in the way his government has used Africanization as a cover for corrupt practice and the subsequent expansion of an African bourgeoisie. Then, as the state emerged as a resource to be plundered, competition for political office intensified and violence, sometimes to the point of murder, became part of normal business (Von Holdt, 2014). Meanwhile, as the incompetent have achieved office and resources have been diverted, so public services have suffered and protests have increased. In other words, while formally democratic, the post-colonial state in South Africa has become a problem.

It obviously was not meant to be like this. An African majority government dominated by the ANC in alliance with the PC and COSATU would, in the context of a modern democratic state with the usual separation of powers and safeguards, transform the life of the masses. Granted, it was not dealt the most promising hand. The international ideologues of globalization, aka neo-liberalism, made their voices felt with an ANC which, in the context of the breakup of socialism as we knew it, had lost its confidence if, deprived of any previous access to office, it had much to begin with. There was also a huge overhang of debt from the apartheid days. As it tried to cling to power, the National Party had borrowed extensively on world markets and now the creditors, having propped up a racist regime, came calling.[10]

But this was the way it has been. One result has been skepticism about the future of democracy in the country, a universal suffrage and separation of powers notwithstanding. The major concern has been the electoral predominance of the ANC; that its rule has become entrenched, supported by a seemingly unassailable majority, and that it therefore lacks the sort of competitive incentive that would allow it to be more responsive to the voters and less prone to corruption.

This might now be changing. It has recently lost ground, particularly in the major cities, but at the national level, and until very recently, it has been dominant (Grootes, 2021).[11] The vote in the 2024 legislative elections has put it in a minority, collecting just over 40% of the total and it has been forced into a government of national unity that includes representatives from the Democratic Alliance: a white dominated party. The white press and the stock market have enthused about this, but this says more about their racism than a sober assessment of the country's future.

The other worry has been the checks and balances supposed to have been effected by the division of powers. The new constitution led to changes in the way in which judges have been appointed. Historically they were made following recommendations by senior members of the bar to the Minister of Justice who then made recommendations to the president. Now it is a matter of the Judicial Service Commission. Just over a third of its members are from the legal profession and the remainder are essentially government appointees, though three of the total of twenty-three have to be from opposition parties. There have been two very different cases, casting doubt on its independence.[12]

---

10 https://www.pambazuka.org/governance/south-africa-apartheid-debt-and-reparations. (Accessed July 7, 2024).

11 In the national election of May, 2024, it has lost its absolute majority vote, and, if it is to govern again, it will be as part of a coalition.

12 One involved a certain Judge Hlophe, who had tried to privately sway two members of the Constitutional Court to dismiss a corruption case against Jacob Zuma. There was suspicion that Zuma had promised him the position of Chief Justice. A disciplinary committee of the Judicial Services Commission then dismissed the complaint. The second case involved a visit to South Africa to attend an African Union summit by Sudan President Omar al-Bashir. While the International Court of Justice (ICC) had issued a warrant for his arrest on grounds of genocide in Darfur, the South African government gave him diplomatic immunity, sidelining its obligation to the ICC. It then ignored a unanimous ruling by the North Gauteng high court that he remain in South Africa, partly on grounds of a supposed ICC bias against Africa and the need to protect South Africa influence in the rest of the continent (see Siyo and Mubaginzi, 2015).

These criticisms of the ANC-dominated state need to be put in context. You do not need a party whose electoral future is secure to feel left out and unable to exercise leverage on government; nor even a grand coalition government. Regardless of which party has ruled in the United States, the poor have always been ignored. The same applies to women in numerous of the advanced capitalist countries; their concerns about childcare, domestic violence, and the economic challenges of single parenting are still in need of serious addressing.

As for the separation of powers, it was ever thus. The three branches are inevitably imbued with social bias, and now the social bias has shifted. The fact that it is racial might seem to make it different, but how different is it from the British case where a particular class establishment rules all three branches? The British judiciary might seem independent because there are few if any signs of direct interference, but to what degree is that because there is no reason to interfere? And the reason that there is no need, is because of a shared class formation that results in decisions that, by and large, do not rock the establishment boat.

3 South Africa and the International Division of Labor

If South Africans of color are to liberate themselves from white domination, in all its dimensions, economic, political and cultural, then there has to be a very substantial expansion of the country's wealth: a material base that would allow both the development of Africans and the creation of a relatively autonomous economic pole in the world economy. Obviously, all these go together: mutual relations between growing autonomy, wealth producing capacities of the economy, and the development of the masses. Furthermore, they depend on an expansion of the country's industrial base.

The prospects here, regardless of the country's internal politics, are not auspicious. In part this is because of an inherited position in the global division of labor which will be difficult to overcome. In part it is because of the circumstances and lasting implications of the conjuncture that has prevailed: that second globalization that has undermined the creation of macro-economic conditions of a propitious sort at the national level; and which has also been the occasion for the rise of China as a most formidable competitor in the race for industrialization. Both of these circumstances are well rehearsed in the literature. The other condition of note has received less attention. This is the matter of geographic location. South Africa is about as far from world markets as it is possible to be. It is partly its location in the southern hemisphere, but also the fact that sub-Saharan Africa, and despite a rapidly growing population, is such an unpromising prospect from the standpoint of selling things. On the other hand, the export performance of other Southern hemisphere countries, some of which are South Africa's peers, has been vastly better and this has translated into increased national incomes (Figure 5).

Re-launching growth after the retreat experienced during the twilight of apartheid is proving much more difficult than might have originally been anticipated. Growth has been relatively slow. During the 1990s it barely kept up with population increase. It approached much more respectable levels after 2000 as a result of the commodities boom and the hunger, particularly in China and India, for minerals of all sorts, but now, in a context of global slowdown, it risks falling back once again. Not surprisingly with this as background, unemployment rates have remained depressingly high and the same goes for poverty rates.

So how might we explain this rather discouraging outcome? I want to consider first the very real dilemmas that the South African government has had to face; dilemmas which any South African government would have had to face, for the degrees of freedom have been extraordinarily limited in so many different ways. This raises the issue of the particular approach that the ANC-led government has adopted in trying to work within those limits and how, again,

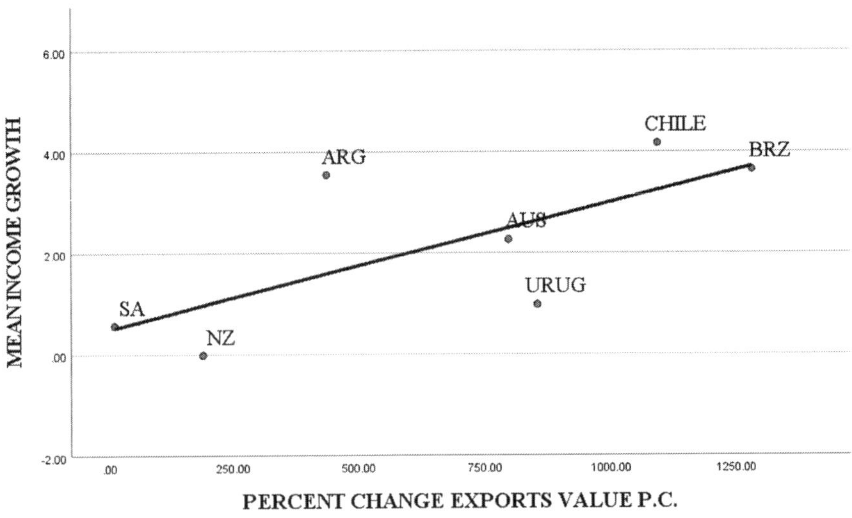

FIGURE 5 Mean income growth and mean export per capita growth, 1970–2020. R = 0.705. Country captions: ARG: Argentina; AUS: Australia; BRZ: Brazil; NZ: New Zealand; SA: South Africa; URUG: Uruguay

DATA SOURCE: HTTPS://DATABANK.WORLDBANK.ORG/SOURCE/WORLD-DEVELOPMENT-INDICATORS# (ACCESSED JULY 9, 2024)

it did not have much choice. I will then conclude with the results of that policy and how we might explain them.

3.1 *'Old' and 'New' Globalizations*

One way of describing the context within which South African governments must work is in terms of the institutional deposits and effects of successive rounds of globalization. The first one that I have highlighted and which I called 'the first globalization' transpired from about 1875 to the outbreak of the First World War in 1914. It was accompanied by rapid expansion of world trade and overseas investment and the sedimentation of a particular international division of labor; one in which the more developed countries of Western Europe and North America provided industrial products in exchange for raw materials. In many instances, the raw-material function was intimately bound up with a colonial presence. This was true of South Africa which, as we have seen, inserted itself as a producer of gold. There was some industrial development later, partly as a result of isolation from the usual suppliers of industrial products during the two world wars and partly as a result of government attempts to diversify the economy. But again, gold continued to prevail until very recently when its preeminence was overtaken by that of other minerals, notably platinum and coal.

One way of grasping this has been the idea of a minerals-energy complex or MEC (Fine and Rustomjee, 1997; Fine, 2008). This refers to an interlocking set of arrangements between mining corporations, and state corporations existing in various upstream or downstream relations: so Eskom which supplies an extraordinarily energy intensive mining industry with electricity, but which itself draws hugely on the country's coal mining. Fine and Rustomjee argue that the MEC has always been a major influence on state policy, both under apartheid and after. One can challenge that as it applies to the apartheid era. While dependent on migratory labor, it could be argued that in that regard, it was simply an inadvertent beneficiary of the apartheid government's ultimate goal of whitening South Africa through expelling Africans to the homelands. Low electricity prices were historically significant for a minerals industry heavily dependent on them. Eskom's recent difficulties in keeping up with demand might suggest some erosion of the significance of minerals in the country's economic base. But Table 16, comparing its major exports in 2000 and 2020 suggests otherwise. The significance of gold in 2020 is surprising but owes in considerable part to a massive increase in the world price: over 450%. On the other hand, and to be discussed further below, it used to be far more significant: over 50% round about 1980, and still at 30% as recently as 1990 (Fine and Rustomjee, 1996, p. 86).

TABLE 16 Major exports by percent of total value

	2000	2020
Platinum	11.3	11.9
Gold	7.1	12.8
Diamonds	5.1	4.7
Coal briquettes	5.0	6.2
Cars	3.5	5.1
Ferroalloys	3.5	2.8
Iron ore	1.9	4.0

SOURCE: HTTPS://OEC.WORLD/EN/PROFILE/COUNTRY/ZAF? (ACCESSED JULY 7, 2024)

Regardless, a difficulty with such a lop-sided form of development is that the demands made on skills development are very modest. Accordingly, it does not lay down a good basis for diversification into progressively more demanding forms of industrial production. Production for the domestic market is also limited since the wages paid in mining have always been lower than in industry, in part because of the relatively unskilled nature of the work and the limited training required, so competition for jobs has been more intense.

The second problem with a minerals emphasis is that it makes a country vulnerable to depletion. During the earlier part of the twentieth century this was a genuine concern of the British colonial authorities, and then of the South African government. It was one of the reasons that migratory labor was viewed as a preferable way of providing the mines with labor (Dubow, 1989). Permanent settlement, it was thought, would create serious problems of adjustment once the gold deposits ran out. If workers were migratory, there would always be a subsistence alternative in the countryside to which they could retreat.

In fact, the pessimism turned out to be unjustified and the industry was given added life after the Second World War with the discovery of new reefs in the Western Transvaal and the Orange Free State. But that good fortune now seems to be running out. In 1984 the gold mining industry employed over 450,000 unskilled personnel. Twenty years later that had shrunk to 130,000; in other words, by a remarkable 71%. From peak production in 1970, the decline in production since then has been precipitous (Figure 6). The same applies to

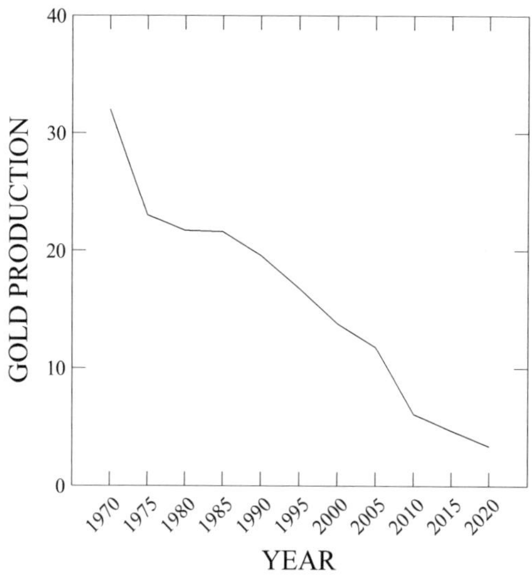

FIGURE 6 Gold production in South Africa, 1970–2020
SOURCE: HTTPS://WWW.MINING.COM/WEB/WORLD-RUNNING-GOLD-MINES-HERES-INVESTORS-CAN-PLAY/COMM-SOUTH-AFRICA-GOLD-OUTPUT-STEADY-DECLINE-MORE-THAN-45-YEARS-10272017-LG/. (ACCESSED JULY 9, 2024)

South Africa's share of world production (Figure 7). From 70% in 1970, it has declined to a mere 4%.

These declines are in part an expression of the physical difficulties now faced by the mining industry. South African gold mines tend to have an increasingly adverse cost profile due to the greater depths at which new deposits are found and the decreasing grade of the ore. These costs have also gone up in virtue of the increasing wages negotiated since the unionization of black miners in the early 1980s. As Feinstein (2005, Chapter 9) pointed out, this has only been in part a result of unionization. Due to uncertainties about recruiting labor from what had become the 'front line states', the mining companies turned more to the South African labor market, where they had to compete to some degree with industry.

As a result, from the state's standpoint the hunt is on for new exports. These are needed in order to pay for South Africa's imports, particularly those of oil, machine tools, transportation equipment like airplanes, medical and IT

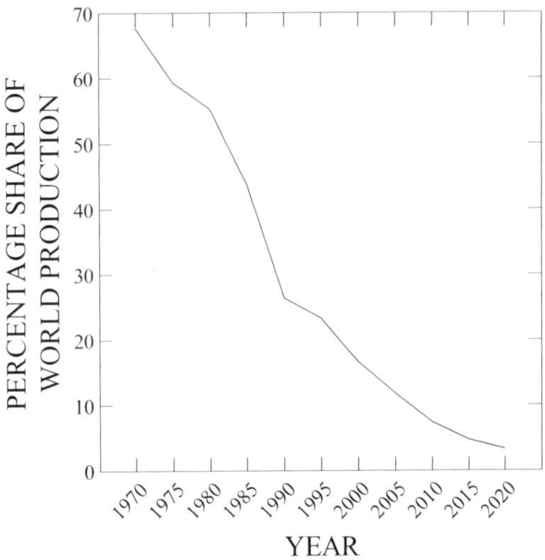

FIGURE 7 South African gold production as a share of world total, 1970–2020
DATA SOURCES: SOUTH AFRICA PRODUCTION: SEE SOURCE FOR FIGURE 6
WORLD PRODUCTION: HTTPS://WWW.RESEARCHGATE.NET/PUBLICATION/306373684_PEAK_OIL_AND_PEAK_GOLD_-_THE_PUNDITS_GOT_PEAK_OIL_WRONG_BUT_PEAK_GOLD_MAY_BE_HERE_BY_MICHAEL_THOMSEN/FIGURES?LO=1 (ACCESSED JULY 9, 2024)

equipment, and luxury goods like the expensive end of the automobile market. Other minerals like platinum and coal have helped, and tourism now accounts for about a tenth of the country's foreign exchange earnings. But what the country needs if it is to increase its wealth and so provide an economic platform for African uplift are more skills-intensive activities that can generate new manufacturing exports.

On the other hand, transforming a mineral-dependent economy into one more focused on industrial growth for overseas markets is a daunting task. The whole social and physical infrastructure of the economy, its knowledge base, its skill structure, the structure of its domestic markets, the various expertises that can be commanded there, are geared towards, or dependent on, mineral production. It is what South African business, whether the mining companies themselves, or the banks which fund them, know best. Furthermore, a good deal of industrial production and its infrastructure depends on minerals (Fine and Rustomjee, 1997). As noted, abundant coal was parlayed into cheap electricity and this was attractive to the refiners of aluminum – a process that is electricity-intensive – even though South Africa has none of the bauxite from which aluminum is ultimately derived. Other industries had a more serendipitous origin. Without the threat of a cut-off from foreign oil suppliers during apartheid it is doubtful that South Africa would have developed the extraction of oil from coal. But they did and for a while, it was a major industry.

To aggravate matters, South Africa has had to try to transform its economic base in less than propitious circumstances. These have been ones of the new or second globalization which became increasingly apparent from the 1980s on. South Africa now had to compete on a global scale and in many different ways. Among other things one would have to note the following:

1. Competition for foreign investment: South Africa's low rate of savings would make foreign investment of interest anyway. There are other reasons. The hope has been that foreign investment will be the conduit for the introduction of new, state-of-the-art technologies; also that integration into the global divisions of labor of industrial multi-nationals or access to overseas distribution networks would open the door to an increase in industrial exports. But this is the dream of most middle-income countries like Brazil, Chile and Mexico. South Africa does not have the field to itself. It also has to compete for the investments of its own corporations. One of the effects of the dismantling of apartheid was that South African firms became welcome investors in foreign countries. Part of this, though, simply reflects the drying up of investment opportunities in some areas in South Africa itself. South African Breweries took over the American brewing company Miller, but if it was to increase its gross revenues, it had to since the domestic beer market was showing signs of weakness.

Africa has become a particularly favored sphere for the expansion of South African firms; sugar plantations in Tanzania, supermarket and hotel chains throughout Southern Africa, mining in Southern, Central and West Africa. In some cases, the moves are directly related to the decreasing profitability of gold mining in South Africa. In others it is a matter once more of the saturation of the South African market. Supermarket chains are now entering the townships but they find the various capital cities and capitalist enclaves scattered across Southern Africa far more attractive than, say, a location in the former homelands. But whatever the reason, the multinationalization of South African business is another condition for the increasing concern about attracting other corporations to invest in South Africa and to limit the flight of others.

2. The competition for foreign investment is a competition for what one might call long term money flows; the money comes in, is embodied in physical plant, and is then recouped through the sales of what is produced using that physical plant and possibly, though not necessarily, repatriated. There is also a competition for short term money flows. One of the necessary conditions for globalization as we know it was the dissolution of the so-called Bretton Woods agreements. By imposing relatively fixed exchange rates linked through the dollar to gold, along with limits to the convertibility of foreign currencies into each other, speculative activity around short term financial flows was very limited. This has now changed. Currency values are determined by supply and demand and large amounts of money are to be made from speculating on future movements. Maintaining the value of the currency has become an important macro-economic goal. With inflation, the costs of imports increase and so, therefore, does the cost of living, there is pressure on labor costs, on the costs of those producers who rely on imported inputs, and so on. To the degree that inflation seems to be taking off, the demand for the currency in question will lag, its value will fall, and inflation will indeed take off.

This has encouraged the pursuit of macro-economic policies of a more austere kind. Interest rates are held above the level that would apply otherwise and by discouraging investment and borrowing for consumer purchases, including housing, this takes demand out of the domestic economy; which is another reason that exports have become such a compelling issue in the second globalization. And in that regard foreign investment is better than domestic, since it increases the demand for the domestic currency and keeps the traders at bay.

South Africa has been affected by this and it has indeed pursued deflationary policies that have been one of the forces discouraging investment in the country. To some degree it has been affected more than most by these logics. This is because, with a black-majority government, it has had more to prove to the currency-trading fraternity. It is also an African country with all that that conveys about political instability, despite the fact that South Africa has been far from unstable, at least until recently; and worst of all, it has suffered from the negative halo cast by its neighbor Zimbabwe.

3. The brain drain: Globalization is many things aside from the increasing predominance of multinational corporations and intensified inter-state competition for their branches and the vertiginous increase in international currency trading. The highly skilled have become footloose, perhaps on a scale not witnessed before. As noted in the last chapter, the development of relatively cheap air travel, e-mail, Zoom, cheap international telephone connections and

the web for 'staying in touch' with friends and relatives back home have all contributed to the relative ease with which people with some technical capacity relocate across international borders, particularly if they have one of the major world languages. And of course, corporations and governments often play an active role in this through their recruitment programs. For some countries, it is a matter of 'brain circulation': benefiting as much as losing. For others, however, including South Africa, the movement has been more one-way and, therefore, disadvantageous, particularly for a country with a serious skills deficiency.

In South Africa, the brain drain is seen as a major problem: an ongoing focus for the media. Some of the numbers mentioned can be quite staggering. According to an earlier report in the Johannesburg Sunday Times for every three British doctors registered in the United Kingdom there is one South African-trained physician. Likewise, South Africa supplied the second highest number of overseas-trained doctors to New Zealand after Britain, and the second-highest number of African graduates to the US after Nigeria. It is not surprising, therefore, that many of the health clinics built in the deep rural areas have suffered from lack of personnel. This is not an issue applying only to the health professions. The restrictions on international movement resulting from the Covid pandemic, led to a big drop in the numbers leaving, but they are now picking up once more.[13] This is something that affects all branches of the economy and state employment too. It includes all population groups though whites predominate and are certainly to the fore in terms of the publicity accorded the brain drain.

4. There is also something quite discouraging that South Africa shares with other middle-income countries. This is Dani Rodrik's (2016) well-documented claim that manufacturing can no longer be the lever that it was for the first-generation industrial countries, notably of North America and Western Europe. Rather, while there can be modest industrialization, de-industrialization seems to be setting in before comparable per capita incomes have been attained. The point at which industrial employment peaks seems now to be much lower. For the United Kingdom it was 45% but now there is a suggestion that India and China will not make it beyond 15%. The suggested reason is the massive advance in productivity in manufacturing which, in terms of generating employment, gives it a much-reduced bang for its buck, unless that is one gives serious consideration to sharing out the product. Thus, according

13 ca/south-africa/south-africa-s-great-brain-drain-28704. (Accessed July 7, 2024).

to one estimate[14] South Africa reached its manufacturing employment peak in 2004, with an income per head about a quarter of that for the US when it achieved the same benchmark. It is hard to work out what the proportion of the workforce in manufacturing actually was in that specific year, but in 2001 it was 14.7% and by 2014, 11.3%; so somewhere around 15% perhaps. Given the transformative role played by industrial proletariats in the West, this has other undesirable consequences; not the least in the South African case, it puts a limit on the social base of any left leaning political party that might emerge in the future.

Rather, and for the foreseeable future, South Africa's role in the international division of labor seems to be more in the direction of what has been called 're-primarization': an increased emphasis on the export of raw-materials, and in South Africa's case, minerals. Tourism slots into the same emphasis. This has been the case with other, similar economies in the Southern Hemisphere. Substantively one can point to the soy boom in Argentina, Brazil and Uruguay; iron ore exports from Brazil and increased exports of copper from Chile, though New Zealand seems to be an exception (Table 17).

But what is particularly worrying about South Africa is that while consignment to primary exports does not necessarily mean an inability to raise living standards, in South Africa, it does. Drawing on the same set of Southern Hemisphere countries, the record is quite dismal (Figure 6 above). Much of this has to be owing to the decline of gold from the 1970s on, but more recently a deteriorating physical infrastructure, as we will see in the final chapter.

3.2 *The Neo-liberal Project*

'Globalization' is often equated to the neo-liberalization of national economies. This means a shift in the boundary between state and market, though quite how this occurs has varied. The privatization of state companies has been common; likewise private tendering to provide public services hitherto provided by the state. There is usually a move in the direction of the so-called de-regulation of the economy; reducing 'red tape' and eliminating layers of bureaucracy. It has meant in addition, an alteration in the balance between business and labor. This was one of its hallmarks in the US and in the United Kingdom under Reagan and Thatcher. There has also been an important international dimension. Trade barriers have been reduced, if selectively, foreign investment encouraged and currencies made convertible. All this has been

14 'Arrested Development: The model of development through industrialisation is on its way out,' *The Economist*, October 2, 2014.

TABLE 17 Percentage share of raw materials in exports

	1990	2000	2010	2020
ARGENTINA	32.6[a]	33.3	28.7	34.2
AUSTRALIA	48.8	41.1	59.6	59.3
BRAZIL	21.4	19.7	42.2	54.0
CHILE	27.2	33.1	36.5	52.2
NEW ZEALAND	43.0	33.0	31.1	34.3
SOUTH AFRICA	17.9[b]	21.6	27.6	29.3
URUGUAY	30.8[c]	32.9	49.9	56.9

a 1993
b 1992
c 1994
SOURCE: HTTPS://WITS.WORLDBANK.ORG/COUNTRYPROFILE/EN/COUNTRY/WLD/YEAR/2000/SUMMARY. (ACCESSED JULY 7, 2024)

with a view to recharging national economies subsequent to the onset of the long downturn discussed in Chapter 4. There is, however, no necessary equation of globalization to the neo-liberal route. The Newly Industrializing Countries of the Far East also opted for export-led growth but their approach was quite different and involved considerable state orchestration. Significantly, South Africa's choice has been the neo-liberal one. Even so, all neo-liberalisms are singular and this is no less true of South Africa. Just why the neo-liberal road was chosen also demands discussion. South African style neo-liberalism is certainly sufficiently so to warrant the label. There has been a very significant liberalization of trade. The idea was to open up South Africa to competitive forces so as to stimulate productivity-increasing investment and make its industrial exports more competitive on world markets, though the effect in some instances, particularly the garment industry, has been retrenchment and increased unemployment. The national currency, the rand, has been made convertible. There have been attempts to privatize some state companies and these are ongoing though there has been significant popular opposition in the case of water and electricity. Now, given their parlous state, it would be hard to find buyers.

One of the things that makes neo-liberalism South African style most distinctive is the continuing position of the African labor movement in the ruling coalition. The ANC has an alliance with COSATU, the Confederation of South African Trade Unions and the government has repeatedly stepped back from a confrontation with them for fear that they might sponsor the formation of their own South African Labour Party. Some evidence of the power of the labor unions has been the difficulty encountered by the South African government in developing a policy of enterprise zones. Through the (highly) localized provision of generous tax considerations, exemption from customs duties on imported raw materials so long as finished products were exported, and exemption from some aspects of labor law, it was believed that South Africa might land some major foreign investments with the capacity to generate employment. The crucial labor law aspects, however, were stripped out as a result of union opposition. Changes in the structure of the South African state have not helped either. The independent homelands, in competing for foreign investment, had their own labor and tax policies and were commonly vigorously anti-union. Whatever the other merits or demerits of these initiatives, they did succeed in attracting some employment-generating activity. With the abolition of the homelands, and the homogenization of labor law throughout South Africa, there have been plant closures and increased unemployment. This is not to call for the return of the homelands; merely to indicate the general principle of some adaptation of policy to massive variations in the cost of living in different parts of the country with a view to attracting desperately needed new investment.

On the other hand, the neo-liberal route, even one that is as qualified and watered down as South Africa's, is not the only way of confronting the challenges of globalization. The idea of the developmental state nurtured by Japan and the common route to industrialization in East Asia, is one that has been widely discussed in South Africa and which has some important advantages over the neo-liberal road. It would, however, be hard to implement under South African conditions, even while there were earlier moves in that direction (Freund, 2019).

The principle assumption behind the developmental state model is that, as a vehicle for promoting industrialization, and in a context where already-developed countries are well ensconced in global markets, reliance on market forces has serious limits. Accordingly, state regulation of trade has been a major feature of the developmental state but not just the control of imports.[15] Another hallmark has been state encouragement in the colonization of

15 The recent discourse of the developmental state had as its context, the rise of the Newly Industrializing Countries in East Asia. See in particular, Amsden (1990).

particular niches in the international market; ones that in virtue of their cost structure, perhaps, appear vulnerable to competition from less industrialized countries. A major vehicle for pursuing this goal has been state allocation of cheap loan finance to firms with the 'right' products in exchange for commitments to export targets. To the degree that the targets were missed, then there would be no more cheap loans. But in addition, as industrial experience was acquired, so the niches targeted would change, using the same methods of discriminatory lending, and with a view to entry into sectors characterized by higher levels of value added; more lucrative sectors from the standpoint of profitability and wages. One implication of this strategy is that inward investment by multinationals has not been encouraged. This is because such firms typically have their own agendas conflicting with those of the developmental state: perhaps a desire to locate only the least skilled parts of their labor process there and with no interest in the upgrading of skill levels.

At the same time, developmental states have carefully protected what advantages they might potentially enjoy in world markets. Wage rates are to the fore. Labor unions have been discouraged, not to say banned, and historically the developmental state has not been friendly to democracy, though with the achievement of a certain level of development, labor movements have acquired more power and the state has been democratized. This has been the story in both South Korea and Taiwan.

One can quickly see the advantages that this particular model of development might offer South Africa. Not least, it could be used to advance the decolonization agenda by setting training targets for firms in exchange for loan finance; or export subsidies in exchange for reaching those training targets. But the necessary conditions for putting a developmental state in place in South Africa just do not exist and it is surprising that it is still being considered. In the first place it assumes that the banks are state owned. Only then can the state intervene in the terms on which low-cost loans are made and insist on export targets as the condition for obtaining further financing. Likewise, it is very unlikely that South African labor union movement would agree to some restrictions on its powers in the interest of promoting the development of the country. Yet subordinating labor to a developmental vision is an absolute *sine qua non* of the developmental state route. What you do have in South Africa, and contrary to the privatizing impulse of neo-liberalism, are state-owned utilities: electricity, railways, ports, the flagship airline. But as we will now see, this has turned out to be a very poisoned chalice indeed.

CHAPTER 6

Zim-Lite?

1 Context

The neo-liberal form of globalization generated a distinct vocabulary: relatively anodyne terms like 'Newly Industrializing Countries', 'de-industrialization', 'outsourcing', and 'privatization'; but also ones with a sharp polemical edge, like 'business climate', and most notably, 'failed state.' This was in the context of the rapid expansion of the multinational presence and of interstate monetary flows of all sorts, both long and short term.

What 'failure' amounts to in this particular understanding of the world includes shortcomings in the rule of law, difficulties in imposing civil order, deteriorations in social provision and in physical infrastructure, sometimes strong centrifugal movements opposing the existing state. 'Failed' states have difficulty managing the national economy and achieving balance both externally and with respect to their own spending. Resort to a bailout from the IMF is, in consequence, a common indicator of 'failure.' This benchmark is provided by the advanced capitalist states of the world, and the fact that it is a conception originating there, speaks loudly about their interests in the matter as well as how they conceive things. This is a classic case of Foucault's power-knowledge but in a world where countries seek to develop on the Western model, one that helps us understand what is going on.

Famously, Sub-Saharan Africa is an area of the world picked out by the risk analysts as one of 'failed' states, including Zimbabwe. South Africa invites comparison in virtue of the fact that they are both settler societies, even while the racial balance favored the settlers far more. They also developed very similar racialized institutions and staggeringly unequal divisions of the land. What has been defined as 'tribalism' is characteristic of both. On the other hand, South Africa is far more developed, is complicated by the presence of a strong intermediate layer of Coloreds and Indians and has a much longer way to fall. There are certainly symptoms of failure in South Africa. But there are also signs of a bourgeois resilience which promise a case of more qualified failure:[1] in other words, more a matter of 'Zim-lite.'[2]

1 Despite the popular pressures, the South African government has repeatedly balked at land expropriation without compensation as part of its land reform policy and has discouraged land occupations: both in sharp contrast to Zimbabwe.

2 Thanks to Jeff McCarthy for suggesting this label.

 | DOI:10.1163/9789004715585_007

2 The Symptoms

2.1 *Infrastructural Collapse*

It was a common view prior to 1994, that South Africa, a middle-income country, had a physical infrastructure more appropriate to a much wealthier one; people talked about a 'first world infrastructure.' This was certainly to ignore the fact that for the vast majority of the population, it served no purpose since they could not access it. The electrification of the townships only started after the early-80s; otherwise, people were still cooking on coal fires, lighting with paraffin lamps, and using batteries to operate radiograms. A major problem is that while there has been increasing demand, simply maintaining and then expanding the physical legacy have not kept up.

A major – huge – case in point is Eskom, the state-owned electricity provider. In 2019 it was producing less electricity than in 2007. Meanwhile, it had taken on more workers.[3] Only recently has there been recognition that the replacement of white engineers with their long experience, by equally qualified Africans, but new to the job, was a mistake. On the other hand, this has only so much to do with Eskom's quite massive debt overhang. In part it is a result of failures of municipalities to pay their bills,[4] owing not just to customer resistance to paying, in their turn, their bills to the municipality, but also the diversion of electricity revenues elsewhere in municipal accounts. There are also big losses from illegal hookups to informal settlements.[5] Plans for expanding supply rested heavily on the construction of two new power stations, Medupi and Kusile, but there have been huge cost overruns tied to bloated BEE (Black Economic Empowerment) tendering. Corruption has been rife.[6]

Given the centrality of electricity to a modern economy, this has massive knock-on effects. It interrupts water supply, including pumping water up to the high plateau on which the Vaal Triangle and the Rand are located. This then means problems in sewage treatment and health problems.[7] And just how do

---

3 Grootes, S. (2019) 'Twelve years of load shedding – written, starring and directed by the ANC.' *Daily Maverick*, December 9, 2019.

4 The municipalities buy their electricity from Eskom, and then serve as the direct retailer to users.

5 Grootes, S. (2022) 'The culture of non-payment in a dysfunctional state.' *Daily Maverick*, February 14, 2022.

6 van Diemen, E. (2023) 'Filthy seam of sabotage – how thieving cartels are plunging South Africa into darkness.' *Daily Maverick*, March 4, 2023. And Harding, A. (2023) 'South Africa load-shedding: the roots of Eskom's power problem.' *BBC News*, May 24, 2023.

7 Fihlani, P. (2023) "South African taps run dry after power shortages." *BBC Online*, June 19, 2023.

you operate a mine at great depth without electricity to circulate the air, to bring workers up to the surface and to take them down? You can install your own backup generator, but at no insignificant cost. The same applies to hotels, restaurants and the tourist trade, which is of no mean importance in South Africa.

The financial situation of other state owned enterprises responsible for much of the country's infrastructure has become equally dire, either declaring bankruptcy, like South African Airlines and South African Express, or dangerously flirting with it: not just Eskom, but the South African Nuclear Energy Corporation, the Petroleum Oil and Gas Corporation, PRASA, responsible for rail transport; not to mention soft infrastructure organizations like the Land and Agricultural Bank of South Africa and the South African Broadcasting Corporation. Public hospitals are in a state of collapse.

Meanwhile, the vandalization of infrastructure has become a massive problem. Anything metal is vulnerable to theft: road signs, manhole covers, the copper in utility cables. In the Johannesburg area the commuter rail system has been reduced to a total wreck and a media cause célèbre, accompanied by photos of dramatic destruction: stations that are a shell, tracks that no longer exist since they have been torn up; something so utterly exceptional as to astound.[8] As far as passenger service goes, this has effects that are utterly regressive. The better-off have cars, but those less so are left to the mercy of exploitative taxi companies.[9]

It is not just the looting. Maintenance and expansion of the physical infrastructure have simply failed to keep up with demand. This has had incalculable effects on production, exports and investment. Timely delivery of minerals to the ports is a pipedream.[10] But most dramatic of all have been failures of electricity supply. Blackouts – so-called 'load shedding' – is something that business now has to confront. Firms install their own petrol or diesel driven generators and the big mining companies are now developing their own sources of solar power, but this is costly.[11] This is a problem that extends beyond what is typically regarded as physical infrastructure to embrace elements crucial for

8 Google 'South Africa vandalization of railway network' and go to Images. Utterly staggering.

9 Makhaye, C. (2023) 'KZN commuters deal with skyrocketing travel costs, unemployment as Prasa network lies in ruins.' *Daily Maverick*, July 13, 2023.

10 Stoddard, E. (2022) 'Flailing Transnet has cost South Africa R50bn ($2.55) in lost mineral exports this year.' *Daily Maverick*, October 5, 2022. See also Mahlaka, R. (2022) 'Ailing Transnet on the brink of becoming South Africa's next Eskom.' *Daily Maverick*, October 16, 2022. And Economist (2023) 'South Africa's collapsing railway company is a cautionary tale.' *The Economist*, January 20, 2023.

11 For some precise figures, see Mahlaka, R. and Moodley, N. (2023) 'South Africa risks becoming a failed state, warn business leaders.' *Daily Maverick*, May 28, 2023.

the reproduction of labor power, not least hospitals where there is a similar litany of woe. Meanwhile, the minerals-energy complex, so historically significant to South Africa's development, is fading away with little to replace it.[12] It is not just the unreliability of the physical infrastructure, it is also that the energy has become hugely more expensive.[13]

According to R. W. Johnson (2021), failures in infrastructural provision are then leading to 'a stampede away from reliance on the state.' Gated communities are a popular response to a public safety provision that is problematic, but also the living place environment in general: so roads that get mended and sidewalks that are maintained. Some of these new developments are striking in their extent and the facilities that they embrace. Steyn City north of Johannesburg has plans for a heliport – why risk your life from a carjacking on the way to the airport? – and a university.[14]

Private sector alternatives are booming. According to Ivor Chipkin (2016, p. 225), there have been major investments in private hospitals, so that they now make up more than a fifth of all hospital beds. Failing electricity systems are met by the installation of solar panels or private generators, failing water supply by an increase in the sinking of boreholes. Private security is a boom sector of the economy. In the context of a now substantial black middle class, these tendencies are decidedly non-racial.

2.2 *Social (Dis)Order*

The issue of public safety / crimes against property in South Africa has long been proverbial, though the looting of the railways is quite recent. Since 1994, and according to all statistics, the crime rate in the country has soared: murder, rape, assault, burglary, car jackings, 'organized' crime,[15] have become part of the staple diet of those who read the South African press. Just how to interpret the figures is something else. The murder rate is the eighth highest in the world.[16] It may be that for blacks, crime has been an ever-present and that the publicity now given it is simply because whites are now more exposed, as

---

12 Stoddard, E. (2022) 'SA mining production tanks 10.4% in year to October, the latest sign of a terminal decline.' *Daily Maverick*, December 13, 2022.

13 Mining Editor. (2023) "Rise of electricity tariffs brings worry to SA mining industry." *Sub-Sahara Mining & Industrial Journal*, January 16, 2023.

14 Thanks to Felicity Kitchin for referring me to this.

15 According to a report in the Mail and Guardian, 'Rough Justice', May 29, 2000, "South Africa's organized crime problem now ranks second only to that of Colombia and Russia."

16 36.4 per 100,000. By way of comparison, France and the United Kingdom are at 1.2 and the US at 4.96. This is not just a matter of relative development. The murder rate in countries

police resources have been redistributed away from white areas to the under-policed townships.

Having said that, just to visit South Africa is to convince that there is something qualitatively different about it. The personal security measures in wealthier neighborhoods are quite extraordinary: burglar bars are standard as are electronically operated gates (operated from inside the house) to admit cars, and even metal gates inside the house separating the bedroom from the living area. High walls surrounding the house and garden are also very common. When you go to park your car to shop or to go to a restaurant, the chances are that someone will step forward and ask if he can watch over your car while you are gone: these are the 'car guards' so pervasive in South Africa, though an expression not just of crime but also of what some people have to do in order to make ends meet. When you go to the bank you step in off the street into a little glass-sided cubicle, the inside door of which is locked; only after you have been looked over (usually discreetly) does the door open; and of course, if there is still a bank robbery, the robber can be detained within the outer cubicle by locking both doors automatically. Drive down any street in a more affluent neighborhood, and it is like moving between two walls. Then, as you pass building sites you will see the measures taken to keep out trespassers looking to pilfer material and equipment: not just cyclone fences but barbed wire. And where construction materials have not been secured then you are likely to see some of the locals happily shoveling sand into wheelbarrows and carting it away.

One response has been vigilantism. Vigilante justice has a long history in South Africa and has not been an African monopoly. The state-sanctioned white commando units long exercised what amounted to powers of arbitrary arrest, detention, and even punishment. The most recent and most widely publicized instances, though, have been identified largely with Africans, and also with Coloreds in the Cape Town area. This corresponds to what is widely perceived to have been an upsurge in crime and a failure on the part of the police and the criminal justice system to contain it: another instance of weakness in state capacity. The results can be horrific.[17]

Some of the violence is directed by Africans against immigrants from the rest of the continent. This is not necessarily spontaneous but is often orchestrated

like Bolivia, Peru, India and Zambia is far, far lower (https://worldpopulationreview.com/country-rankings/murder-rate-by-country.) (Accessed July 9, 2024).

17 See Heywood, M. (2022) 'Death penalty returns to SA through mob murder – with spike in deaths due to blunt force injury, say doctors.' *Daily Maverick*, May 29, 2022.

by political movements which have tried to exploit tensions around small business and housing. The most notorious of these is something called Operation Dudula. Extortion, trashing of immigrant-owned shops, arson, seizure of stock, death threats to lawyers defending the immigrants, eviction from abandoned buildings: these are all part of its modus operandi. This has then had knock-on effects for the economy in general, like truck drivers blocking major routes to push a demand that immigrants not be hired for the same employment.

The violence extends to small business. The taxi cab industry is viciously competitive and routes are defended through gunfire and murder, and if the passengers get in the way, too bad.[18] Informal, often illegal activity, is highly vulnerable to extortion under the threat of violence. Such has been the lot of the so-called 'zama zamas', many of whom are immigrants, often undocumented, who dig in abandoned gold mines for a pittance at great physical danger and are then subject to threats from rival groups or middlemen who demand a share of the loot.

A recent development has been the construction mafia. Often going under seemingly progressive names like the Federation for Radical Transformation or the XX Youth in Action Movement, they demand jobs or a share of the contract in exchange for refraining from violence: in short, protection money, and targeting white and African companies alike. Moreover, it is not necessarily small business like the taxi companies that are at risk. Platinum mines in Mpumalanga have been targeted by so-called 'business forums' through roadblocks as a means of extracting more jobs for locals. The business forums and chiefs then compete, often violently, for the spoils.[19] This is to omit reference to the farm murders. Much publicized by the Afrikaner farmer organizations like the Transvaal Agricultural Union, these are often carried out without anything stolen, suggesting that they are revenge killings, and labor relations on white farms often have an ugly history. These are now on the decline but as a percent of all murders in South Africa, the number was always derisory: scarcely more than a third of a percent.

In fact, it is Africans by far, and then in the Western Cape, Coloreds, who are likely to feel the brunt of the orgy of violence. Whites may live far away from it, and, in virtue of their money, can, like businesses, call on the private security industry. This is a veritable 'growth sector' in the South African economy. Corporations are big employers of private security guards. The wealthy

---

18 Brody, P. (2021) 'South Africa: Shootings and revenge killings in latest 'taxi war' attacks.' *France24*, July 7, 2021.

19 Stoddard, E. (2022) 'Fear, loathing and extortion on the eastern limb of South Africa's platinum belt.' *Daily Maverick*, July 3, 2022.

TABLE 18 South Africans resident abroad

2000	501,600
2005	550,462
2010	743,807
2015	786,554
2020	914,901

SOURCE: STATSSA (2024) MIGRATION PROFILE REPORT FOR SOUTH AFRICA: A COUNTRY PROFILE 2023. PRETORIA

can take advantage of the full panoply of electronic monitoring, external walls, large, automatically controlled, iron gates, and alarm systems, or the gated community. In short, they have the power to deter. The vast majority of the population has to depend on the police. And to the degree that the wealthy do in fact deter criminals in these ways, then the crime gets shifted in the direction of those who can only react after the fact.

2.3 *'Exit'*

Moving into a gated community is one way of escape, but the likelihood is that you still have to leave to go to work. The alternative is movement on a grander scale. The Western Cape has been the retreat par excellence. Over the period from 1996 to 2019, its share of the country's white population increased by over four percentage points, where it was already one of the whitest and was certainly the least African of all the provinces.

The alternative to the Western Cape or Gauteng – also increasing in its share, but more modestly – is overseas. The outmigration of whites has been considerable. South Africa's white population reached a peak in 1995 (5,224,000.) It has since declined by over ten percent. Table 18 is indicative of a growing stream. Take an airplane from the US to South Africa and there will be more than a modest sprinkling of émigrés on their way to visit family. There has been white immigration, but mainly wealthy retirees from the United Kingdom looking for cheaper living by the sea in Cape Town.

The other way of escape has been more obviously political: redraw the political map of South Africa so that part of it now goes missing. This is the goal of the Cape Independence Party. It would create an independent country of the provinces of the Western and the Northern Cape and small contiguous municipalities of the Eastern Cape and the Free State that, significantly, have an Afrikaans-speaking majority[20] and where Africans are in a minority. The Western Cape has long been the one province where the ANC has struggled to form the provincial government. In the provincial elections of 2019, with 55.5% of the vote, the white-dominated Democratic Alliance (DA), albeit with significant Colored support, obtained almost twice the number of votes as the ANC. In the election of 2024, the ANC fell even further behind: 19.6% of the vote to the DA's 55%. Thus far, the appeal of separatism has been very limited, even while the Cape Independence Party claims that a majority of supporters of the DA are in favor of a referendum to support a breakaway.[21] But the very fact of its existence is significant, as have been official calls by the provincial DA for devolution.[22]

3 Towards an Explanation

Assuming the continuing dominance of the capitalist form of development, if there is to be serious redistribution and mitigation of the crushing poverty of very, very large numbers indeed, much rests on growth, and therefore on the accumulation process; or at least, that has always been the fundamental premise of South Africa's ruling class. But infrastructural collapse and widespread social disorder make that prospect more and more daunting.

A crucial condition for the current situation in South Africa, is precisely that poverty and in many, highly mediated ways. People struggle to make ends meet; hope is a luxury. The crime mafias, the so-called business forums, the widespread alienation and violence, the attacks on non-Africans, make little sense otherwise. The same applies to the widespread corruption that undermines not just the economy but the legitimacy of the South African state, even while it helps legitimize other extra-legal activities. Lacking this desperation, including that of the office holders for whom the alternatives are often dim indeed, it would be much harder to fathom. This, though, is not enough. There is something more fundamental still, and that is the fact of the post-colonial

20 This is not, however, a synonym for 'white' since the Coloreds also tend to be Afrikaans-speaking.

21 The Referendum Party, its formal political expression, received a derisory 0.26% of the total vote in the 2024 election.

22 Mpofu-Walsh, S. (2022) 'DA flirts dangerously with Western Cape separatists.' *Mail and Guardian*, October 24, 2022. And Steenhuisen, J. (2022) 'The revolution has failed. Let's try devolution.' *News24*, November 1, 2022.

both in the state and the social relations that subtend it and which it then informs.

In the very early post-apartheid years, there was optimism. While shaken by the lead-up to the collapse of apartheid, South African capital looked forward to the security that the new regime could provide: pacification was a major step forward. Its major corporations were largely home grown, and had very significant investments not easily cast aside. But two things happened. The first was that the country's growth prospects were dimmed as neo-liberalism ran riot. Persuaded to join the World Trade Organization and adherence to its strictures led to eliminating industrial protection; which then decimated the textile industry and the employment it had provided. Capital controls were dismantled, facilitating outward investment: not unreasonable given the limitations of the domestic market and old ambitions blocked by the sanctions placed on the apartheid regime. The hope of course was that this outward investment would be balanced by movement in the opposite direction. Then major firms, like Anglo American, as it then was, Old Mutual, Barlow World, Mondi and Illovo, delisted from the Johannesburg Stock Exchange in favor of London, ostensibly to deepen the capital markets which they could access. Finally, there was the shareholder revolution which meant increased distributions and less money for investment (Prins et al., 2018, Chapter 2).

The second thing was that South African capital remained, in its ownership and management, very white. This was so partly in virtue of obstacles thrown in the way by apartheid law to the entrepreneurial ambition of Africans.[23] There was very little in the way of a domestic African capitalist class on which to build. Furthermore, and despite the equal opportunity subsequent to the dismantling of apartheid, the corporate world remained a closed one, lubricated by long familiar relationships and prejudices.

This would have two results. The first would be, on the part of the government, a sharpening of the sense that the country needed a black capitalist class. And second, there would be a racial division of labor between the economy and the state: the former, predominantly white and the latter, African. The state would then emerge as a theater in which Africans could make money, by means both fair and foul.

23 Indians are an interesting contrast. They have been the big gainers from the ending of apartheid, not just because of the better education facilities made available to them under that regime, but also because their business activities were not limited by law as were those of Africans. There was always a substantial Indian business class. Interestingly, this logic does not seem to have applied to the same degree to the Colored population.

The principal lever for creating an African capitalist class would be Black Economic Empowerment or BEE. Select Africans – don't ask how they were selected – would be granted on a delayed purchase scheme, big blocks of shares in corporations with the assumption that their increasing value would pay for them.[24] The formation of this class would then be further promoted through the preferential tendering policies of state departments and parastatals. The possibilities for this were enhanced by the fact that much remained under state control: electricity, public utilities, railways, airports, docks, the national airline – exactly the providers of the physical infrastructure that has experienced implosion.

If 'neutral' administrators had been in charge, a civil service 'above politics', i.e., not with a capital 'P', things might have worked out differently. But to advance its public agenda of developing the country and raising all boats, the ANC wanted ideological alignment. This was the justification given for what would be known as cadre deployment: inserting its own people, even while, as it would turn out, they lacked the administrative experience and technical nous necessary to run a public utility. This would set the scene for major corruption on the part of the African political class, at all levels of the state, national, provincial and municipal, and a very different politics from that which might reasonably have been anticipated.

For the rapid growth of labor union membership among Africans in the last twenty years of the apartheid regime, along with the radical aspirations of the ANC as it then was, might have suggested that once apartheid was out of the way, class politics would flourish. Clearly this has not been the case. It is not just that electoral politics has amounted to a racial census: Africans divided between a dominant ANC and the Economic Freedom Fighters or EFF; whites, Indians and Coloreds largely for the Democratic Alliance, though with an increasing number of African professionals. Rather politics, at least for the ANC and EFF, has tended to degenerate into something quite orthogonal to an organization around class interests of a universal sort: a labor movement, that is, that joins the working classes everywhere into a solidaristic movement aiming at collective uplift against a wealthy moneyed class aiming to protect and to expand their wealth at working class expense. It is, rather, a politics organized more vertically around a multiplicity of competing factions whose leaderships are bent on mobility of an individualistic sort, and pulling in their wakes networks of clients. There *is* a more clearly class element: the Democratic

24 A big bet as it turned out, since the anticipated rise in share prices on the South African stock exchange did not materialize.

Alliance is certainly more focused on the preservation of material privilege.[25] But they have not been a feasible alternative government. At the last election in 2024, they managed scarcely 22% of the vote, and that is unlikely to change in the immediate future; which helps to explain why the party has continued to agitate for a devolution that would give them more independence in their Western Cape heartland. African politics, therefore, can persist as exactly that, and in a happy security from outside challenge, unless, that is, DA participation in the new government of national unity can actually make a difference. It is a politics, moreover, that has tended to be replicated in the labor unions, which is not surprising given that the union federation, COSATU has continually committed its support to the ANC.

To expand: Two important features define this politics. First, it is one of patronage, in which politicians and public officials cultivate a support base peculiar to themselves and in a variety of ways, both big and small. An elected official in charge of a government department can favor particular businesses in their tendering for services, in its decisions over licenses, and access to land for mining companies. But, and particularly at local levels, it can be a matter of services: the allocation of government housing, the upgrading of highways, the installation of flush toilets in a township, the hiring of school teachers.

Second, it is an extraordinarily corrupt politics. This assumes a dazzling variety of forms: outright nepotism and embezzlement certainly, but the big stuff typically involves kickbacks in exchange for tenders for state contracts. Elective state office is seen as the gateway to wealth enhancement, often spectacular; which is a major reason for factionalism in the ANC and election campaign violence (Von Holdt, 2014.) It can also be a way of putting together the resources through which to ascend the political hierarchy and so to gain access to even bigger prizes. A classic case is David Mabuza,[26] Vice-President from 2018 to 2023, who was the Prime Minister for the province of Mpumalanga for nine years. During that period he diverted money from the provincial government intended for the schools to building a support base for the provincial ANC, signing up members in exchange for jobs, money, even meals. This put him in control of the biggest block of ANC members in the country; significant

25 But far from exclusively white. In fact, it is supported by Africans, Coloreds and whites in almost equal proportions and the support of most of the Indians: https://www.da.org.za/2022/09/turning-point-diverse-da-now-the-biggest-political-party-in-urban-south-africa. (Accessed July 9, 2024) . While this is a party political document, the data were derived from an independent source.

26 Onishi, N. and Gebrekidan, S. (2018) 'South Africa vows to end corruption. Are its new leaders part of the problem?' *New York Times*, August 4, 2018.

in the election of party leaders. This then meant that he could act as kingmaker for the election of the current president, Cyril Ramaphosa, and secure his own access to loot on a still grander scale.

This, again, has been true at all levels of the state, national, regional or local. But to gain office, the aspirants need a personalized support base and they need to offer it something. This makes for a highly factionalized politics, and a constant threat to party unity. The party is merely a vehicle for the enhancement of personal fortunes, which means that those in office are under constant threat from those seeking their own disgruntled support base in an effort to secure election. At the local level, the frustrations of those in the vast spread of informal settlements can be taken advantage of. As one settlement is favored, so another is left behind, spawning demands, blockades of roads, destruction of property in protest, and generating the interest of those who can exploit the anger for their own, immediate, electoral purposes (Dawson, 2014): what Beresford (2015) has described as 'gate keeper politics' in which the existing gate keepers are constantly challenged by rivals keen to usurp their privileges. But at the local level, the stakes for the voters are increased as a result of the fact that, by law, local development projects must hire local contractors and local workers.

This is the content of democracy as it is currently practiced in South Africa. There are no formal democratic controls in the tribal authorities, but the situation there is similar. With restitution of land, a new institution has been required, a Community Property Association or CPA. While the land is communally owned, there have been tendencies for tribal leaders to arrogate control of these Associations to themselves and a tight coterie of kin. Nepotism in appointments, obscure distributions of rents from those working the land[27] or of royalties from mining companies have been typical (Nxele, 2022). Tribal leaders are bribed by mining companies eyeing extraction possibilities. The mining companies then encroach on communal land, fencing it off, appropriating water resources and common grazing land, reducing the subsistence prospects of the many (Zamchiya, 2022). Contestation of these practices by those affected is then met with violence.

27 For example, Timse, T. (2015) 'Conflict erupts over Limpopo CPA control.' *Mail and Guardian*, August 10, 2015; Broughton, T. (2021) 'Millions of rands in suspicious transactions found in accounts of Limpopo land claimants.' *GroundUp*, August 18, 2021; Ngomane, T. and Sebola, M.P. (2020) 'Agrarian reform and communal property associations: an analysis of the functionality of CPA's in Mpumalanga,' The *5th Annual International Conference on Public Administration and Development Alternatives* 07 - 09 October 2020, Virtual Conference, University of Limpopo.

This is a politics that is, remarkably enough, replicated within the union movement. Positions of authority provide opportunities for the receipt of bribes, embezzlement, the award of pay increases, and kickbacks for those supplying services to the union: printers, cleaners, among others. But also opportunities for upward mobility: "The trade unions, much like other sections of the liberation movement, have witnessed a 'race to riches' in which leadership positions have become stepping stones into political careers or lucrative private-sector opportunities. This has increased the social distance between union officials and the rank and file" (Beresford, 2015, p. 151).

This then generates the same sort of factionalism as in the ANC. Mass alienation sets in, creating the conditions for a breakaway union but led by those smelling the possibility of personal advancement; which then compromises any sense of class unity. Union leaderships jockey for one in the ANC: the story of Ramaphosa and ultimately of Marikana as former union leaders, now invested in business, turn against the working class.

The obvious contrast is with the role played by the unions under the COSATU umbrella in the struggle against apartheid: a 'social movement unionism' which set it clearly against South Africa's privileged. Since then, affirmative action and the elimination of job reservation has led to an increasing differentiation of salary in the unions, particularly between the skilled and the unskilled. According to Beresford (2016, Chapter 4), this is seen largely as a generational divide: the more skilled, educated young, against the less skilled older workers, with less social capital; a divide that is intensified by tendencies to outsource their jobs.

Violence in politics rules, though more clearly in that of the ANC than of the labor unions: something emphasized in Von Holdt's work. Street barricades, the bombing of local councilors' houses, the burning down of libraries, schools and other symbols of authority are common.[28] Competitors for public office and whistleblowers risk assassination. The conflicts are zero-sum and the stakes can be huge. The alternative to the perks of office can be bleak; likewise, failure to secure the election of a favored candidate who has promised to deliver, and particularly so for the masses who live day to day with little hope.

Accordingly, one of the ways of understanding what is happening is in terms of the extraordinary inequality in the country and the fact of an immensely poor sub-proletariat, unemployed, clinging to a precarious foothold in the city and living hand to mouth through the so-called 'informal economy', from the

28 A recent example here, Hirsch, M. (2023) 'Swellendam community centre burnt down as residents rampage over electricity hike and indigent policy.' *Daily Maverick*, September 20, 2023.

pensions of a grandmother, and petty theft. They, particularly the young, are available to riot, to protest the lack of services, and to support, violently if necessary, the claims to office of someone who has promised jobs, housing, a tender that will generate jobs, or whatever. Nor can one divorce what is happening from the masculinist nature of African society. Violence is a way of expressing a male agency otherwise denied. It is an expression of the frustration of young men at being unable to put together the money for lobola and form their own household of which they can be the head (Von Holdt et al., 2011). Securing public office is a way out of it; and once secured, you will fight to keep yourself out of the morass, accumulating through corruption for the inevitable rainy day. As R. W. Johnson remarked on the Jacob Zuma era: "Think of the situation of ANC MPs being told to vote for or against Zuma. Many of them know perfectly well that if they put a foot wrong and they lose their jobs, they will be sitting in a shack, unemployed in a squatter camp. They can't fall back on being a lawyer/doctor or whatever. They will actually be unemployed and semi-starving so it's a very desperate situation and people in those situations fight hard."[29]

Second, there is the fact of opportunism. The elimination of the old racial order opened up the prospect of elevation, either hard won, or through the color of one's skin. The rapidity with which the solidarities of the struggle against apartheid were cast aside is simply extraordinary and sheds a severe light on so-called 'ubuntu.'[30] In the advanced capitalist societies, the way in which politics has been conditioned by class interest has certainly weakened and given way to more volatile, fluid forms of identity, but this is a process that has been ongoing for a long time. So is it that it was never a matter of

29 Hogg, A. (2017) 'R W Johnson: ANC's promotion of racist rhetoric has an even darker side. But it won't work.' *BizNews*, 4/21/17, available here: https://www.biznews.com/interviews/2017/04/21/rw-johnson-anc-racism. (Accessed July 9, 2024). Compare Mike Morris (2017): "The critical defining feature of this predatory criminal process, differentiating it from straight organized crime to which it has many other similarities, is that it involves setting up an alternative shadow structure of companies and ownership mirroring these government officials. It is a mechanism of class formation for the economically incompetent who would not survive in the cut and thrust of capitalist competition of the real economy, since they lack the real skills and capabilities required to operate productive enterprises." A substantial number of city and municipal councilors are, in fact, illiterate. For the KwaZulu Natal case see Grill, B. and Schaap, F. (2023) 'The slow and steady demise of South Africa.' *Der Spiegel*, September 8, 2023. Available here: https://www.amren.com/news/2023/09/the-slow-and-steady-demise-of-south-africa/. (Accessed July 9, 2024). And Morris is far from being a conservative voice looking to justify continuing white hegemony. See also Von Holdt (2014) and Suttner, R. (2022) 'ANC crisis may foreshadow its demise and deepen state turmoil.' *Daily Maverick*, November 21, 2022.

30 An African normative ideal emphasizing the fundamental interdependence of people.

class for people of color in South Africa and far more a matter of race? That labor unions always played an ambiguous role? On the one hand, they did indeed represent their members in struggles with management over pay and conditions of work. But on the other, they gave support to a struggle that was about overthrowing a racial minority rather than changing a balance of class power. The idea of a labor movement in the South African context was always an ambiguous proposition, despite the lofty ANC rhetoric of taking the pillars of the economy into public ownership. Is this, in fact, the legacy of what has been described as colonialism of a special type, where a settler minority ruled independently of an imperial power, and had the numbers and economy to be able to do it?

The classical form of capitalist development, as it unfolded in Belgium, France, Germany, Italy, Sweden, the United Kingdom and, to lesser degree in the United States, was one in which the consciousness of class, expressed in the form of a strong labor movement, played a crucial role. Through its workplace demands for improved conditions and higher wages, it stimulated technical development; and as capitalists moved to techniques involving more fixed capital, that too, and paradoxically, tended to strengthen labor's hand since interruptions to production became that much more costly. Again, the labor movement was to the forefront of the drive for the universalization of the franchise, albeit for males only. This would then lead to the creation of a welfare state and further pressures on capital to develop the forces of production.

It is in this context that a very particular national consciousness emerged, albeit alongside that of class.[31] What is 'good for the nation' is structurally entailed in societies of this particular form. Political parties are organized along class lines, but in order for those of the right to win an election, they have to appeal across the class divide to at least some working-class voters. Historically, and until the decline of the labor movement from the mid-1970s on, this made them wary of any attempt to repeal the social gains made by parties of the left. To the extent that the right succeeded in making inroads into the support base of Labour and Social Democratic parties, the same constraints

31 Compare Davidson (2016): "the capitalist system generates nationalism as a necessary, everyday condition of its continued existence. It develops new structural capacities, new modes of experience and new psychological needs in the people who have to work in the factories and live in the cities. It is this need for some collective sense of belonging with which to overcome the effects of alienation, the need for psychic compensation for the injuries sustained at the hands of capitalist society, that nationalism provides in the absence of revolutionary class consciousness, but in conjunction with reformist class consciousness".

had their effect, as Przeworski (1980) made clear. In this process, you could not appeal in blatant, undiluted class terms; rather it had to be in terms of some notion of the national interest, and this notion tended to congeal around the national economy and what to do about it. The emphasis on the right might be on growth and on the left, on 'fairness' but these were never defined in strictly class terms. Growth was supposed to lead to the raising of all boats. 'Fairness' applied to everyone and became a national value; treating everyone 'fairly' – so an empty signifier that could be made to do a lot of work, and sometimes useful work. There was a balance of forces apparent in the alternation of the parties as the parties of government, which encouraged compromise around a shared growth policy, tilting more to one side now and then more to the other.

In countries like South Africa, that are 'deeply divided', this trajectory is far less feasible: no class compromise because the vast majority do not define politics as a matter of class interest. Race is a zero-sum game, putting any notion of a national economy in which all have a stake, if a different one, to one side. The ANC might appeal to some whites, it is, after all, supposed to be non-racial, but the emergence of groups like the Economic Freedom Fighters is a harsh reminder to toe the racial line or risk election losses. In class conscious societies, compromise is structurally entailed, even if it is a compromise that works to the advantage of capital; there is always the hope that with the return of the left to power, the balance might shift. In South Africa, this is not the case. As we have seen, voting in South Africa still approximates a racial census. Likewise, there can be no national history; no shared conception of what South Africa means. For whites it means one thing and for people of color, something entirely different; utterly opposite, as befits a people long oppressed by the white minority. The mutual trust that facilitates a socialization of production embracing all, regardless of race, is hard to achieve. Suspicion grows like the proverbial weed.

South Africa is often compared with Brazil. There are similarities: racial hierarchy, similar levels of development, high levels of corruption, an extractive economy, and major social disorder. But there are also important contrasts which shed light on the peculiarities of the post-colonial in South Africa. In Brazil there is a clear class politics; a class divide over the issues that always divide in a self-consciously class society: a strong versus a minimalist state, the magnitude of the welfare state, of the real minimum wage, and a government that alternates between a workers' party and one clearly on the side of the moneyed classes. In the twentieth century, the right to vote has never been explicitly along racial grounds, or even covertly. Illiteracy was a bar until 1988 but never linked to race. The idea that Brazil is a non-racial society is part of the national mythology.

For the longest time, Brazil and South Africa fought for the dubious distinction of being the most unequal country in the world. Table 19 suggests that this is no longer the case. The statistics are uneven but it would seem that the two countries have moved in opposite directions since the turn of the century, and despite an alternation in Brazil's governing party. Perhaps more interesting, though, is the case of Bolivia, where inequality has gone down very significantly indeed. Since 2006, and with a break of less than a year, the governing party has been in character and self-definition, socialist: MAS or, in English, the Movement for Socialism.

Bolivia, in terms of the usual indicators of development is on a clearly lower level than South Africa. The GDP per capita (PPP) in 2022 for South Africa is almost two-thirds higher.[32] On the other hand, there are some similarities of a structural sort. There is what looks like a similar racial hierarchy: those who can claim a European origin sometime in the past, are to the whites of South Africa, the indigenous Indians to the Africans, and the mestizos to the Coloreds. In more strongly white areas, notably cities like Santa Cruz and Cochabamba, the stigmatization of the Indians is especially strong. The Indian highlands are an important source of migratory labor for the big farms in the lowland east, and there are drives for the redistribution of land. One could even make out a case for a similarity between the push in the lowland east for greater autonomy, even independence – and similar pressures in the Western Cape. But from the point of view of the postcolonial state, and interestingly, these similarities do not seem to be very relevant. Bolivia is apparently different, which is an important reason for why there has been an impressive decline of inequality there, and without generating a serious backlash.

So, how to explain? And what light does it shed on the South African case? First, the racial-cum-ethnic balance is very different (Table 20): *Movimiento al Socialismo* or MAS, which has superintended a raising of incomes of the poor, could not be effective as a party representing purely the Indian population; mestizo support is crucial to it obtaining a majority of legislative seats (Centellas, 2016, p. 13). Moreover, ethnicity is only part of the picture in understanding voting in Bolivia, since there are strong, cross-cutting regional divides (Pila, 2014; Hirseland and Strijbis, 2019). Significantly, the weight of history is different: since 1952, there have been no racial restrictions on the right to vote. In this, the ANC stands in sharp contrast: a raison d'être in the struggle for the right to vote; and since then, an electoral situation in which it can win purely on the basis of the African vote.

32 https://data.worldbank.org/indicator/NY.GDP.PCAP.PP.KD.

TABLE 19 Gini coefficients 2000–2020, Bolivia, Brazil and South Africa

	2000	2002	2004	2006	2008	2010	2012	2014	2016	2018	2020
BOL	61.6	59.3	55.0	56.7	50.8	46.1[a]	46.6	47.8	45.2	42.6	43.6
BRZ	58.4[a]	58.1	56.5	55.6	54.0	52.9[a]	53.5	52.0	53.3	53.9	48.9
SA	57.8	n.d.	n.d.	n.d.	63.0	63.4	n.d.	63.0	n.d.	67.0[b]	n.d.

a Plus or minus a year
b https://africacheck.org/infofinder/explore-facts/what-was-south-africas-gini-coefficient-2020. (Accessed July 9, 2024)
SOURCE: HTTPS://DATA.WORLDBANK.ORG/INDICATOR/SI.POV.GINI (ACCESSED JULY 7, 2024)

TABLE 20 Ethnic composition, Bolivia, South Africa

	Bolivia	South Africa
Indian / African	20%	80.2%
Mestizos/Coloreds and (Asiatic) Indians	68%	11.3%
Europeans	5%	8.4%

SOURCE: WIKIPEDIA. (ACCESSED JULY 11, 2024)

Like South Africa, Bolivia is an extractive economy, relying heavily on its hydrocarbon sector and on the agribusiness of the eastern lowlands. The former has been crucial to the government's success in raising the masses out of poverty and reducing inequality in the country. It helped that the government was able to take it back into public ownership without local opposition, since it was largely under foreign control. Increased taxation on the industry has then made possible a doubling of government investment in the public infrastructure: hospitals, schools, and highways, the construction of which allowed an increase in wages. Increased general prosperity then made possible a quadrupling of the minimum wage between 2005 and 2019, and the creation of a universal pension program. Land reform has occurred, initially through the expropriation of privately owned land in the east, and giving farm workers title; but later, and significantly for reducing political tensions around the program, confining retitling to state owned land. In short, redistribution without a serious rocking of the political boat (Wolff, 2019).

While Bolivia's trajectory has been dramatically different, that of Brazil, less so. But they both share a similar post-colonial transition. For a very long time, the settler hegemony has been muted by the fact that the formal barriers to political participation, to state office, if at lower levels, have been non-existent. In South Africa, with some minor exceptions like the black municipalities of the 1980s, from the standpoint of Africans there has been utter discontinuity, so that the takeover of a highly sophisticated state apparatus, contained the very real possibility of failure. Elsewhere, and not only in the advanced capitalist world, there has been a slower, more organic build-up of state capacities, of lines of communication with civil society, of systems of recruitment and training and advancement. Under the post-colonial conditions of South Africa, radical rupture made this very difficult. The long-excluded now dominate the state apparatus and the civil service, but they have very limited experience. Little wonder that the 1994 agreements did not work to their advantage Meanwhile a white capitalist class loses confidence in political leadership and can point in justification to the decay of the country's physical infrastructure and a social order that is fragile to say the least.

South Africa now seems caught in a downward spiral. The orgy of cannibalization of the public infrastructure feeds back to undermine production and investment. Demand for South African minerals has boomed but getting them to the ports by way of rail is difficult. Electricity is unreliable and there are numerous instances of malfunctioning of the health system. Discouragement leads to a skills drain. There is little in South Africa to encourage the investment so sorely needed if the condition of the masses is to improve.

•••

I am by no means the first to raise the specter of a failed state in South Africa. Others have already made the case (Boraine, 2014; Johnson, 2015; Cronjé, 2020).[33] One can certainly criticize the idea. It serves the purposes of the multinationals as they scout the world for investments, and is promoted in a self-serving way by the governments of the advanced capitalist countries. This is so, even while they themselves can be judged as 'failed' in their own ways. 'Failure' though, in the particular forms it assumes in South Africa is a daily

33 Though as one might anticipate, this is a contested view. The term 'fragile' has been offered as an alternative as here, Derby, R. (2022) 'South Africa is not a failed state, but we are fragile.' *Mail and Guardian*, February 6, 2022.

reality for those living there, and something to which they struggle to adapt. It seriously diminishes life chances, and the ability to adapt is sharply unequal. If you have the money for your own electricity generator, to drill your own well, and are able to live in a gated community with access for your children to the better schools, fine; but the vast majority, particularly of Africans, are not in that situation.

Few would have anticipated this outcome back in 1994.[34] Certainly the settlement was in many ways an unfavorable one for African majority rule. Pressures were brought to bear by the experts to ensure that the country would be safe for capitalism, proposals that were eagerly taken up by the still hegemonic representatives of 'white' South Africa and accepted by a resistance movement eager to assume power: so a commitment to pay off the international debts of the apartheid regime, to protect property rights, to forego expropriation without compensation, and then, weirdly, a commitment to open up the national economy to the neoliberal flavor of the day. From the standpoint of African emancipation on both political and economic fronts, national conditions were disadvantageous from the start. Labor intensive industries faced crushing competition from, dominantly, Chinese firms. White business made its own adaptations: expelling Africans from white farms from fear of land claims; and de-listing on the Johannesburg stock exchange for a flight to the London one in search of investors skittish about the rand.

This might have been expected. What was not, was the reneging on the commitments that the ANC leadership had made to its followers. There have been modest improvements to lives but scarcely enough to numb the effects of a devastating lack of formal employment. Rather for the ANC the state has been seen as the road to personal enrichment, running down the country's infrastructure, physical and social, and creating an environment of violence as the struggle for positions in the state intensifies. The divorce of leadership from its social base is nothing new in the social democracies, but the level of overt corruption is.

One can certainly create a post-hoc argument to explain this, but emphatically what has transpired could not have been anticipated. On the other hand, serendipity is always, and paradoxically, structured: history, more accurately

34 But some did, and not just the National Party. These included such varied people as Bill Freund (personal communication) and Margaret Thatcher, even while she pushed vigorously for the end of apartheid. On claims that the ANC feeding frenzy has long roots, see Grill, B. and Schaap, F. (2023) 'The slow and steady demise of South Africa.' *Der Spiegel*, September 8, 2023. Available here: https://www.amren.com/news/2023/09/the-slow-and-steady-demise-of-south-africa/. (Accessed July 9, 2024).

geohistory, matters; and for several centuries now, a capitalist geohistory. The capitalist form of development matters hugely. It is, as Marx repeatedly claimed, necessarily global. He was not to the point of referring to a global division of labor, or a necessary fragmentation into countries, but they too were necessary. Within that very broad context of possibilities and limits, there have also been those provided by a more concrete geohistory that would have been hard to anticipate. These have included the succession of globalizations highlighted in this book; of technological ensembles as implied by talk of 'first', 'second' and a possible 'third' industrial revolution; and then of imperial forms, from empire, through the more aggressive, violent, forms of neo-colonialism, to what might be called neo-colonialism lite. Class struggle on a global scale has flowed and then ebbed, rather than the other way around, reaching a climax in the first two decades of the last century, stabilizing in the postwar period, and then clearly losing in intensity since the crisis of the 1970s.

In virtue of what was already there in pre-capitalist times, natural conditions, pre-capitalist forms of production relation, settlement patterns, institutional forms, the comings and goings of an increasingly spatially extended capitalism, have then worked to create highly localized, country-specific, sets of social arrangements. What emerged around gold and the nature of those deposits in South Africa is a case in point and recalls Harvey's (1985) claims about structured coherences and how they would be defended, as indeed they were when racially discriminatory practice was called into question. So the global is always thoroughly implicated in what happens in particular countries, and the converse applies. In virtue of the gold standard, the development of gold mining in South Africa was significantly implicated in the growth associated with the first globalization. More recently, the hope of the World Bank was that South Africa would prove to be an exemplar for the rest of the continent.

But regardless of questions of geography, capitalism means that difference is baked in from the start (Cox, 2021, Chapter 10): stories of inferiority, inadequacy of some sort, have fed the discourse through which capitalist ruling classes have asserted their right to organize, to subjugate, to justify colonialism, to appropriate. A necessarily insecure working class has then lent its own weight to these discriminations, and in some cases, coming up with its own. Stratification in capitalist societies has always incorporated ideas of difference and has been impelled to do so; and to the extent that old ones fade away, new ones are created in their place. The early English bourgeoisie thought that those of the working class were genetically predisposed to fecklessness, sloth, improvidence and inebriation and that they needed the civilizing example of their masters; paradoxical, yes, but to the degree that the working class believed in its own inferiority, it worked. That same working class would then, for its own reasons, project those same deficiencies onto the immigrant Irish.

Nationality, race, religion, gender, traditional forms of dress, areas of origin, have all been used at some time, somewhere, to greater or lesser degree. In South Africa it was always race which tended to dominate. In part this reflected the dominant imperialist discourse of the time. In South Africa, though, it was intensified by the peculiar conditions in the gold mining industry; most notably an early and necessary racial stratification of the workforce, where tensions were increased by sharp differences in expectations regarding material standards, and then, as Africans learnt by doing, the attempts of the mine owners to displace the more expensive Europeans.

In short, modern South Africa owes its character to an encounter of peoples differentiated not just by accepted racial features but by very different capacities to impose themselves on each other, and, crucially, in the context of the demands and tensions of the capitalist form of development. This was a development that was always global in its reach, imposing roles in an international division of labor and class struggle on a global scale, if always in distorted forms: earlier in the form of Hyslop's (1999) 'white laborism', and then the long struggle to reverse the challenge of socialist revolution; something that would prolong the agony of the African masses of South Africa.

While one cannot reduce the current conjuncture in South Africa, the flirting with failed state status, to these background conditions, it is incomprehensible without them, and further investigation of the juxtaposition of forces that gave detail to them – the strength of the white presence, a relatively advanced industrialization, the total exclusion of non-Europeans from power – adds force to that point. How to get out of the mess is far from clear. The social forces necessary to launch a counterattack and restore the hopes of the masses are yet to become visible. What should be apparent and drawing lessons not just from South Africa's past but from those of any other country in the world, is that it will take more than domestic change to do the trick. Global circumstances have been not just limiting but also, at certain times, enabling, and even liberating. Currently, and some backlash against its neoliberal form notwithstanding, they do not favor progressive forces, whether in South Africa or elsewhere. One is reminded of Zhou Enlai's famous statement about the French Revolution. He was almost certainly misunderstood, referring to 1968 rather than to 1789, but the general point should be taken. Events, like the displacement of apartheid have a long afterlife, all the consequences of which have been impossible to foresee.

References

Adam, H., Van Zyl Slabbert, F. and Moodley, K. (1997) *Comrades in Business*. Cape Town: Tafelberg.

Amsden, A. (1990) 'Third World Industrialization: 'Global Fordism' or a New Model?', *New Left Review*, 1(182): p. 70–81.

Aronowitz, S. (1978) 'Marx, Braverman and the Logic of Capital', *The Insurgent Sociologist*, 7(2–3): p. 126–146.

Ashforth, A. (1997) 'Lineaments of the Political Geography of State Formation in Twentieth-Century South Africa', *Journal of Historical Sociology*, 10(2): p. 101–126.

Batchelor, P., Dunne, P. and Lamb, G. (2002) 'The Demand for Military Spending in South Africa', *Journal of Peace Research*, 39(3): p. 339–354.

Bénichi, R. (2003) *Histoire de la mondialisation*. Paris: Vuibert.

Beresford, A. (2014) 'Nelson Mandela and the Politics of South Africa's Unfinished Liberation', *Review of African Political Economy*, 41(140): p. 297–304.

Beresford, A. (2015) 'Power, Patronage and Gatekeeper Politics in South Africa', *African Affairs*, 114(455): p. 226–248.1993

Beresford, A. (2016) *South Africa's Political Crisis: Unfinished Liberation and Fractured Class Struggle*. London: Palgrave Macmillan.

Bhorat, H., Naidoo, K. and Yu, D. (2014) 'Trade Unions in an Emerging Economy: The Case of South Africa', *World Institute for Development Economics Research*, WIDER Working Paper 2014/055.

Bonner, P. (1991) 'The Politics of Black Squatter Movements on the Rand, 1944–1952' in Brown, J. et al. (eds.) *History from South Africa*. Philadelphia: Temple University Press, p.59–81.

Bonner, P., Delius, P. and Posel, D. (1993) *Apartheid's Genesis 1935–1962*. Johannesburg: Ravan Press.

Boraine, A. (2014) *What's Gone Wrong? On the Brink of a Failed State*. Johannesburg and Cape Town: Jonathan Ball Publishers.

Bozzoli, B. (1983) 'Marxism, Feminism and South African Studies', *Journal of Southern African Studies*, 9(2): p. 139–171.

Brenner, R. (1998) 'The Economics of Global Turbulence', *New Left Review*, 1(229): p. 1–265.

Burman, S. and Reynolds, P. (1990) *Growing up in a Divided Society*. Evanston IL: Northwestern University Press.

Callinicos, A. (1988a) *South Africa Between Reform and Revolution*. London: Bookmarks.

Callinicos, L. (1982) *Gold and Workers: A People's History of South Africa*, Vol 1. Johannesburg: Ravan Press.

Cavanaugh, E. (2016) 'Settler Colonialism in South Africa', in Cavanaugh. E. and Verancini, L. (eds.) *The Routledge Handbook of the History of Settler Colonialism*. London: Routledge, p. 291–309.

Centellas M. (2016) 'Disarticulating 'Ethnic' Voting in Bolivia's National and Municipal Elections.' Paper prepared for the *XXXIV International Congress of the Latin American Studies Association*, New York, May 27–30, 2016. Available at: https://www.researchgate.net/publication/303315219_Disarticulating_'Ethnic'_Voting_in_Bolivia's_National_and_Municipal_Elections (Accessed June 19 2024).

Charney, C. (1984) 'Class Conflict and the National Party Split', *Journal of Southern African Studies*, 10(2): p. 269–282.

Chipkin, I. (2016) 'The Decline of African Nationalism and the State of South Africa', *Journal of Southern African Studies*, 42(2): p. 215–227.

Christopher, A. J. (1994) *The Atlas of Apartheid*. Routledge: London and New York.

Christopher, A.J. (2009) 'Delineating the Nation: South African Censuses 1865–2007'. *Political Geography*, 28(2): p. 101–109.

Clarke, S. (1990) 'Crisis of Socialism or Crisis of the State', *Capital and Class*, 42: p. 19–29.

Connors, M. K. (1996) 'The Eclipse of Consociationalism in South Africa's Democratic Transition', *Democratization*, 3(4): p. 420–434.

Cox, K. R. (2004) 'Globalization, the Class Relation and Democracy', *GeoJournal*, 60: p. 31–41.

Cox, K. R. (2021) *An Advanced Introduction to Marxism and Human Geography*. Cheltenham, UK: Edward Elgar.

Cox, K. R. and Hemson, D. (2008) 'Mamdani and the Politics of Migrant Labor in South Africa: Durban Dockworkers and the Difference that Geography Makes', *Political Geography*, 27: p. 194–212.

Crankshaw, O. (1996) 'Changes in the Racial Division of Labor during the Apartheid Era', *Journal of Southern African Studies*, 22(4): p. 633–656.

Cronjé, F. (2020) *The Rise or Fall of South Africa*. Cape Town: Tafelberg.

Crosby, A. (1986) *Ecological Imperialism: The Biological Expansion of Europe, 900–1900*. Cambridge: Cambridge University Press.

Crush, J. (1989) 'Migrancy and Militancy: The Case of the National Union of Mineworkers of South Africa', *African Affairs*, 88: p. 5–23.

Crush, J. (1993) 'The Long-Averted Clash: Farm Labor Competition in the South African Countryside', Canadian Journal of African Studies, 27: 404–23.

Crush, J. (1995) 'Mine Migrancy in the Contemporary Era' in Crush, J. and James, W. (eds.) *Crossing Boundaries: Mine Migrancy in a Democratic South Africa*, Cape Town: Institute for Democracy in South Africa, p. 14–31.

Crush, J., Jeeves, A. and Yudelman, D. (1991) *South Africa's Labour Empire: A History of Black Migrancy to the Gold Mines*. Boulder CO, San Francisco and Oxford; and Westview Press; and Cape Town: David Philip.

Davidson, N. (2016) 'State and Nation: An Interview with Neil Davidson', *Viewpoint Magazine*, April 25, 2016 (interviewed by Benjamin Birnbaum).

Dawson, H. J. (2014) 'Patronage from Below: Political Unrest in an Informal Settlement in South Africa', *African Affairs*, 113(453): p. 518–539.

Denoon, D. and Nyeko, B. (1987) *Southern Africa Since 1800*. Harlow: Longman.

Dubow, S. (1989) *Racial Segregation and the Origins of Apartheid in South Africa*. London: Macmillan.

Dutt, R. P. (1936) *World Politics 1918–1936*. London: Gollancz.

Ebersohn, W. (1981) *Store up the Anger*. New York: Doubleday.

Feinstein, C. H. (2005) *An Economic History of South Africa*. Cambridge: Cambridge University Press.

Fine B. (2008) 'The Minerals-Energy Complex is Dead. Long Live the MEC?' Paper presented to *Amandla Colloquium, Continuity and Discontinuity of Capitalism in the Post-Apartheid South Africa*, 4–6 April, 2008, Cape Town.

Fine, B. and Rustomjee, Z. (1997) *The Political Economy of South Africa*. Boulder CO: Westview Press.

Fraser, N. (2000) 'Rethinking Recognition', *New Left Review*, NS(3): p. 107–120.

Freund, B. (1995) *Insiders and Outsiders*. Pietermaritzburg: University of Natal Press.

Freund, B. (2014) 'The Shadow of Nelson Mandela, 1918–2013', *Review of African Political Economy*, 41(140): p. 292–296.

Freund, B. (2019) *Twentieth-Century South Africa: A Developmental History*. Cambridge: Cambridge University Press.

Gelb, S. (1987) 'Making Sense of the Crisis', *Transformation*, 5: p. 33–50.

Gleijeses, P. (2014) 'The United States, South Africa, and the Cold War', *Radical Historian*, 119: p. 236–240.

Gleijeses, P. (2016) *Visions of Freedom: Havana, Washington and Pretoria and the Struggle for Southern Africa, 1976–1991*. Durham NC: University of North Carolina Press.

Goldin, I. (1987) *Making Race: The Politics and Economics of Colored Identity in South Africa*. London: Longman.

Good, K. (1976) 'Settler Colonialism: Economic Development and Class Formation', *The Journal of Modern African Studies*, 14(4): p. 597–620.

Graham, H. (2005) *The Spanish Civil War: A Very Short Introduction*. Oxford: Oxford University Press.

Grootes, S. (2021) 'The ANC will Remain in Power for Many Years After 2024 – Here's Why', *Daily Maverick*, December 1, 2021.

Grundlingh, A. (2019) 'Afrikaner Nationalism in the 1930s and 1940s' in Molapo, R.R. and Mohamed, A. (eds.) *Turning Points in History (Book 4): Industrialization, Rural Change and Nationalism*. Johannesburg: Real African Publishers, Chapter 3.

Hanlon J. (2010) 'How the Cold War Shaped Mozambique Today.' Paper presented at a conference on the *Legacies of Conflict, Decolonization and the Cold War*, Lisbon, May 28–29, 2010.

Harris, L. (1986) 'South Africa's External Debt Crisis', *Third World Quarterly*, 8(3): p. 793–817.

Harvey, D. (2005) *A Brief History of Neoliberalism*. Oxford: Oxford University Press.

Hattingh S. (2007) *BHP Billiton and SAB: Outward Capital Movement and the International Expansion of South African Corporate Giants*. The International Labour Research and Information Group (ILRIG).

Hirseland, A-S. and Strijbis, O. (2019) '"We were Forgotten": Explaining Ethnic Voting in Bolivia's Highlands and Lowlands', *Journal of Ethnic and Migration Studies*, 45(11): p. 2006–2025.

Hobsbawm, E. (1990) *Nations and Nationalism Since 1780*. Cambridge: Cambridge University Press.

Hyslop, J. (1988) 'School Student Movements and State Education Policy: 1972–1987' in Cobbett, W. and Cohen, R. (eds.) *Popular Struggles in South Africa*. London: James Currey, p. 183–209.

Hyslop, J. (1993) A Destruction Coming in': Bantu Education as Response to Social Crisis', in Bonner, P., Delius, P. and Posel, D. (eds.), *Apartheid's Genesis*. Johannesburg: Ravan Press and Witwatersrand University Press, p. 393–410.

Hyslop, J. (1999) 'The Imperial Working Class Makes Itself 'White': White Labourism in Britain, Australia, and South Africa before the First World War', *Journal of Historical Sociology*, 12(4): p. 398–421.

Hyslop, J. (2000) 'Why did Apartheid's Supporters Capitulate? 'Whiteness', Class and Consumption in Urban South Africa, 1985–1995', *Society in Transition*, 31(1): p. 36–44.

Johnson, R. W. (2015) *How Long will South Africa Survive? The Looming Crisis*. Johannesburg: Jonathan Ball.

Johnson, R. W. (2021) 'Thinking About State Failure (III)' *Politicsweb*, March 1, 2021. Available here: https://www.politicsweb.co.za/opinion/thinking-about-state-failure-iii-2 (Accessed July 11, 2024).

Joubert, E. (1980) *Poppie Nongena*. New York: Henry Holt.

Khalili, L. (2023) 'Woke Capital', *London Review of Books*, 45(17).

Klein, N. (2007) *The Shock Doctrine: The Rise of Disaster Capitalism*. Toronto: Knopf.

Lacey, M. (1981) *Working for Boroko*. Johannesburg: Ravan Press.

Lazar, J. (1993) 'Verwoerd Versus the 'Visionaries': The South African Bureau of Racial Affairs (Sabra) and Apartheid, 1948–1961' in in Bonner, P., Delius, P. and Posel, D. (eds.), *Apartheid's Genesis*. Johannesburg: Ravan Press and Witwatersrand University, p. 362–392.

Lijphart, A. (1968) 'Consociational Democracy', *World Politics*, 21(2): p. 207–225.

Maddison, A. (2003) *The World Economy: Historical Statistics*. Paris: OECD.

Mamdani, M. (1996) *Citizen and Subject*. Princeton: Princeton University Press.

Mamdani, M. (2001) 'Beyond Settler and Native as Political Identities: Overcoming the Political Legacy of Colonialism', *Comparative Studies in Society and History*, 43(4): p. 651–664.

Mann, M. (1995) 'Sources of Variation in Working Class Movements in Twentieth-Century Europe', *New Left Review*, 1(212): p. 14–54.

Maré, G. (2005) 'Race, Nation, Democracy: Questioning Patriotism in the New South Africa,' *Social Research*, 72(3): p. 501–530.

Marx, K. (1867; republished 1976) *Capital*, Vol. 1. Harmondsworth Middlesex: Penguin.

McKinley, D. (2023) 'A Tarnished Halo – Reassessing Nelson Mandela's Legacy 10 Years after his Death', *Daily Maverick*, December 12, 2023.

Miliband, R. (1969) *The State in Capitalist Society*. London: Weidenfeld and Nicholson.

Moll, T. (1991) 'Did the Apartheid Economy Fail?', *Journal of Southern African Studies*, 17(2): p. 271–291.

Morris, M. L. (1977) 'State Intervention and the Agricultural Labor Supply Post-1948' in Wilson, F., Kooy, A. and Hendrie, D. (eds.) *Farm Labor in South Africa*, Cape Town: D. Philip, p. 62–71.

Morris, M. L. (1980) 'The Development of Capitalism in South African Agriculture: Class Struggle in the Countryside' in Wolpe, H. *The Articulation of Modes of Production*. London: Routledge Kegan Paul, p. 202–253.

Morris, M. L. (2017) 'Op-Ed: South Africa's Problem is Greater and Deeper than the Guptas, Zuma, and their Cronies', *Daily Maverick*, August 14, 2017. Available at: https://www.dailymaverick.co.za/article/2017-08-14-op-ed-the-problem-is-greater-and-deeper-than-the-guptas-zuma-and-their-cronies/ (Accessed: 19 June 2024).

Murray, M. J. (1994) *The Revolution Deferred*. London: Verso.

Naidoo, V. (2005) 'The State of the Public Service' in Daniel, J., Southall, R. and Lutchman, J. (eds.) *State of the Nation: South Africa 2004–2005*. East Lansing MI: Michigan State University Press, p. 110–134.

Norval, A. (1996) *Deconstructing Apartheid Discourse*. London: Verso.

Notermans, T. (1997) 'Social Democracy and External Constraints' in Cox, K. R. (ed.) *Spaces of Globalization*. New York: Guilford Press, p. 201–239.

Nxele, M. (2022) 'Crony Capitalist Deals and Investment in South Africa's Platinum Belt: A Case Study of Anglo-American Platinum's Scramble for Mining Rights, 1995–2019', *Review of African Political Economy*, 49(173): p. 395–416.

O'Meara, D. (1983) *Volkscapitalisme: Class, Capital and Ideology in the Development of Afrikaner Nationalism, 1934–1948*. Cambridge: Cambridge University Press.

O'Meara, D. (1996) *Forty Lost Years*. Johannesburg: Ravan Press.

Offe, C. (1984) *Contradictions of the Welfare State*. Cambridge, MA: MIT Press.

Ogura, M. (1996) 'Urbanization and Apartheid in South Africa: Influx Controls and their Abolition', *The Developing Economies*, 34(4): p. 402–423.

Parnell, S. (1993) 'Creating Racial Privilege: The Origins of South African Public Health and Town Planning Legislation', *Journal of Southern African Studies*, 19(3): p. 471–488.

Parnell, S. and Mabin, A. (1995) 'Rethinking Urban South Africa', *Journal of Southern African Studies*, 21(1): p. 39–61.

Paton, A. (1948) *Cry the Beloved Country.* London: Jonathan Cape.

Pila, E. L. (2014) 'We Don't Lie and Cheat Like the Collas Do.' Highland-Lowland Regionalist Tensions and Indigenous Identity Politics in Amazonian Bolivia', *Critique of Anthropology*, 34(4): p. 429–449.

Piven, F. F. and Cloward, R. (1971) *Regulating the Poor.* New York: Pantheon.

Platzky, L. and Walker, C. (1985) *The Surplus People.* Johannesburg: Ravan Press.

Plomer, W. (1925) *Turbott Wolfe.* London: Hogarth Press.

Posel, D. (1991) *The Making of Apartheid 1948–1961.* Oxford: Oxford University Press.

Poulantzas, N. (1969) 'The Problem of the Capitalist State'. *New Left Review*, 1(58): p. 67–78.

Prins, N. et al. (2018) *Shadow State: The Politics of State Capture.* Johannesburg: Witwatersrand University Press.

Przeworski, A. (1980) 'Social Democracy as a Historical Phenomenon', *New Left Review*, 1(122): p. 27–58.

Richburg, K. B. (2024) 'Why Some South Africans are Rethinking Nelson Mandela's Legacy', *Global Opinions*, 3/23/24.

Rodrik, D. (2016) 'Premature Deindustrialization', *Journal of Economic Growth*, 21(1): p. 1–33.

Romus, P. (1958) *Expansion économique Régionale et Communauté Européenne.* Leyde: Sythoff.

Saul, J. S. and Gelb S. (1981) 'The Crisis in South Africa', *Monthly Review*, 33(3): p. 1–156.

Seekings, J. (1988) 'The Origins of Political Mobilization in the PWV Townships, 1980–84' in Cobbett, W. and Cohen, R. (eds.) *Popular Struggles in South Africa.* London: James Currey, p. 59–76.

Sayer, A. (1984) *Method in Social Science.* London: Hutchinson Press.

Silver B. (2004) 'Labor, War and World Politics: Contemporary Dynamics in World-Historical Perspective' in Unfried, B., van der Linden, M. and Schindler, C. (eds.) *Labor and New Social Movements in a Globalizing World System.* Leipzig: Akademische Verlaganstalt.

Siyo, L. and Mubaginzi, J. C. (2015) 'The Independence of South African Judges: A Constitutional and Legislative Perspective', *Potchefstroom Electronic Law Journal*, 18(4): p. 817–846.

Smith, D.M. (1982) 'Urbanization and Social Change Under Apartheid: Some Recent Developments' in Smith D.M. (ed.) *Living Under Apartheid.* London: George Allen and Unwin, Chapter 2.

Stengel, R. (1990) *January Sun.* New York: Simon and Schuster.

Taylor, R. (1992) 'South Africa: A Consociational Path to Peace?', *Transformation*, p. 17: 1–11.

Traverso, E. (2016) *Fire and Blood: The European Civil War, 1914–1945*. London: Verso.

Visser, W. P. (2001) 'The South African Labor Movement's Responses to Declarations of Martial Law, 1913–1922.' Paper presented at the *War and Society in Africa Conference*, South African Military Academy, Saldanha Bay, September, 12–14, 2001.

Von Holdt, K. (2014) 'On Violent Democracy', *Sociological Review*, 65(S2): p. 129–151.

Von Holdt, K., Langa, M., Molapo, S., Mogapi, N., Ngubeni, K., Dlamini, J. and Kirsten, A. (2011) *The Smoke that Calls*. Johannesburg: The Centre for the Study of Violence and Reconciliation and the| Society, Work and Development Institute.

Wilson, F. and Ramphele, M. (1989) *Uprooting Poverty: The South African Challenge*. Cape Town and Johannesburg: David Philip.

Wolff, J. (2019) 'The Political Economy of Bolivia's Post-Neoliberalism', *European Review of Latin American and Caribbean Studies*, 108: p. 109–129.

Zamchiya, P. (2022) 'Mining, Capital and Dispossession in Post-Apartheid South Africa', *Review of African Political Economy*, 49(173): p. 417–435.

Index

Printed in the United States
by Baker & Taylor Publisher Services